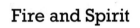

Fire and Spirit

Inner Land

A Guide into the Heart of the Gospel

Volume 4

Fire and Spirit

Eberhard Arnold

PLOUGH PUBLISHING HOUSE

Published by Plough Publishing House
Walden, New York, USA
Robertsbridge, East Sussex, UK
Elsmore, NSW, Australia

Plough is the publishing house of the Bruderhof, an international community of families and singles seeking to follow Jesus together. Members of the Bruderhof are committed to a way of radical discipleship in the spirit of the Sermon on the Mount. Inspired by the first church in Jerusalem (Acts 2 and 4), they renounce private property and share everything in common in a life of nonviolence, justice, and service to neighbors near and far. To learn more about the Bruderhof's faith, history, and daily life, see Bruderhof.com.

ISBN: 978-0-87486-320-8

23 22 21 20   1 2 3 4 5 6

Translated from the 1936 edition of *Innen Land: Ein Wegweiser in die Seele der Bibel und in den Kampf um die Wirklichkeit* (Buchverlag des Almbruderhof e. V.). This edition is based on the 1975 English edition translated by Winifred Hildel and Miriam Potts. Cover image: *Lighted Sky* (oil on canvas) by Erin Hanson, copyright © Erin Hanson. Used with permission.

A catalog record for this book is available from the British Library.
Library of Congress Cataloging-in-Publication Data

Names: Arnold, Eberhard, 1883-1935, author.
Title: Fire and spirit / Eberhard Arnold.
Other titles: Licht und Feuer. English
Description: Walden, New York, USA : Plough Publishing House, 2020. |
Series: Inner land: a guide into the heart of the gospel ; volume 4 |
Summary: "Lightning and forest fires could strike terror in primitive humans, yet they also cherished fire as a life-giving gift from the gods"-- Provided by publisher.
Identifiers: LCCN 2020003925 (print) | LCCN 2020003926 (ebook) | ISBN 9780874863208 (hardback) | ISBN 9780874863215 (ebook)
Subjects: LCSH: Holy Spirit. | Light--Religious aspects--Christianity. | Fire--Religious aspects--Christianity.
Classification: LCC BT121.3 .A7613 2020 (print) | LCC BT121.3 (ebook) | DDC 248.4/897--dc23
LC record available at https://lccn.loc.gov/2020003925
LC ebook record available at https://lccn.loc.gov/2020003926
Printed in the United States

Dedicated to my faithful wife,
Emmy Arnold

Contents

Preface

Born to an academic family in the Prussian city of
Königsberg, Eberhard Arnold (1883–1935) received a
doctorate in philosophy and became a sought-after
writer and speaker in Germany. Yet like thousands
of other young Europeans in the turbulent years
following World War I, he and his wife, Emmy,
were disillusioned by the failure of the establish-
ment – especially the churches – to provide answers to
the problems facing society.

In 1920, out of a desire to put into practice the
teachings of Jesus, the Arnolds turned their backs
on the privileges of middle-class life in Berlin and
moved to the village of Sannerz with their five young
children. There, with a handful of others, they started
an intentional community on the basis of the Sermon
on the Mount, drawing inspiration from the early
Christians and the sixteenth-century Anabaptists.
The community, which supported itself by agricul-
ture and publishing, attracted thousands of visitors
and eventually grew into the international movement
known as the Bruderhof.

Eberhard Arnold's magnum opus, *Inner Land*, absorbed his energies off and on for most of his adult life. Begun in the months before World War I, the first version of the book was published in 1914 as a patriotic pamphlet for German soldiers titled *War: A Call to Inwardness.* The first version to carry the title *Inner Land* appeared after the war in 1918; Arnold had extensively revised the text in light of his embrace of Christian pacifism. In 1932 Arnold began a new edit, reflecting the influence of religious socialism and his immersion in the writings of the sixteenth-century Radical Reformation, as well as his experiences living in the Sannerz community. Arnold continued to rework the book during the following three years, as he and the community became targets of increasing harassment as opponents of Nazism. The final text, on which this translation is based, was published in 1936. Arnold had died one year earlier as the result of a failed surgery.

This final version of *Inner Land* was not explicitly critical of the Nazi regime. Instead, it attacked the spirits that fed German society's support for Nazism: racism and bigotry, nationalistic fervor, hatred of political enemies, a desire for vengeance, and greed. At the same time, Arnold was not afraid to critique the evils of Bolshevism.

The chapter "Light and Fire," in particular, was a deliberate public statement at a decisive moment in Germany's history. Eberhard Arnold sent Hitler a copy on November 9, 1933. A week later the Gestapo raided the community and ransacked the author's study. After the raid, Eberhard Arnold had two Bruderhof members pack the already printed signatures

of *Inner Land* in watertight metal boxes and bury
them at night on the hill behind the community
for safekeeping. They later dug up *Inner Land* and
smuggled it out of the country, publishing it in Lich-
tenstein after Eberhard Arnold's death. Emmy Arnold
later fulfilled her husband's wish and added marginal
Bible references. (Footnotes are added by the editors.)

At first glance, the focus of *Inner Land* seems to
be the cultivation of the spiritual life. This would be
misleading. Eberhard Arnold writes:

> These are times of distress; they do not allow us
> to retreat just because we are willfully blind to the
> overwhelming urgency of the tasks that press upon
> human society. We cannot look for inner detachment
> in an inner and outer isolation. . . . The only thing
> that could justify withdrawing into the inner self
> to escape today's confusing, hectic whirl would be
> that fruitfulness is enriched by it. It is a question
> of gaining within, through unity with the eternal
> powers, that strength of character which is ready to
> be tested in the stream of the world.

Inner Land, then, calls us not to passivity but to
action. It invites us to discover the abundance of a
life lived for God. It opens our eyes to the possibilities
of that "inner land of the invisible" where "our spirit
can find the roots of its strength." Only there, says
Eberhard Arnold, will we find the clarity of vision we
need to win the daily battle that is life.

The Editors

Light and Fire

Light triumphs over darkness

In every epoch of history there have been terrible
calamities and bitter injustices. Faced with the daily
suffering of masses of people, the human spirit has
proved throughout to be cold, indifferent, and insen-
sitive, no matter what appalling depths the misery
reaches. In times of crisis people need a shaking
jolt to see the darkness and coldness lowering over
them. There is no salvation without judgment upon
injustice and unrighteousness. Today's universal and
persistent need drives us to look for the cause. Only
when the debris is cleared away can the source of help
flow freely.

Times of darkness call for faith in light from above. Isa. 60:1–2
Before this light, all darkness will retreat, just as
morning triumphs over every night. The ugliness and Rom. 13:12–13
horror of darkness and its cold, murderous spirits
must penetrate into our consciousness. In utter
helplessness, we must be on watch for the hour of
redemption, for no human being can bring liberation

Luke 21:25–28 or relief. Help must come from the other world if all life is not to sink into the cold night of death. Under this crushing burden of the nightmare of darkness, people need to be given a glimpse of the fire descending from above in liberating light.

The light of faith will shine upon darkness and all-pervading cold. Light triumphs over darkness, 1 John 1:5–7 which is death. Death attacks life. When love grows Matt. 24:12 cold, injustice escalates beyond measure. Darkness hates light, and forced to retreat, it puts up the most John 3:19–20 violent resistance. The brightness of awakening life is terrifyingly painful to all those who have become strangers to strong light. Accustomed to the darkness all around them, they find the blazing glory of light unbearable torture. It burns in their eyes like fire. The victorious light becomes judgment. The radiant flame of life, which demands love, judges the darkness of unpeace and puts to flight the coldness John 12:46 of injustice.

A few days after Pascal's death,[1] a sheet of paper was found in the lining of his suit. He had kept it on him constantly for eight years as a precious reminder of his deepest experience. On this parchment, the shaking description of an overwhelming enlightenment begins with the solitary word: fire. Jesus brought flames of judgment and of salvation. Jesus wanted to kindle a fire, and his greatest longing was Luke 12:49 for it to burn. He brought glowing fire to the earth. But the fire he hands over to darkened humankind is not stolen in sacrilegious theft by a second Prometheus from a jealous deity.[2] God is the giver here.

---

1 Blaise Pascal, 1623–1662, French mathematician and theologian.

2 In Greek mythology, Prometheus steals fire from Zeus and gives it to humanity.

Jesus is the fiery rays of a divine heart that pours out
its fire constantly over all people.

God himself gave his fiery brand into the Son's
hand through his Spirit. The torch of wrath became a
dispenser of life. The flames of judgment became one   1 Pet. 1:7
with life's fire, alive in the liberating and gathering
light of love. Jesus knows what this blazing fire meant
to the fearful heart from the beginning of history,
what trembling and terror it brought upon the erring
tribes. He knows that there is no fire without the
judgment that consumes what is dying – withered and   2 Pet. 3:7–10
hardened life.

The fires of heaven and the fires of the deep –
flames of lightning falling from heaven and volcanic
fire bursting out of the earth, forest giants burning
like pillars of fire and fiery missiles from the glowing
breath of mountains, lightning that strikes fire with
rolling thunder and lava from the quaking earth
setting fire to everything in its path – filled early man
and all creatures of the earth with shuddering awe.
People shook with deadly fear at the immeasurably
superior, all-powerful might of this blazing wrath.

Before this fire can show radiant warmth and
protecting, uniting power, the flames of its wrath
must be revealed as consuming judgment. The flames
of God's heart shall cause dread before they disclose
their ultimate purpose. The prophet could not help   1 Cor. 4:5
trembling with fear lest he lose his sight in God's
heavenly fire by looking with impure eyes at the God
of the shining Hosts. God himself says, "You cannot   Exod. 3:6
see my face, for no one may see me and live!" We have   Exod. 33:20
fallen too deep into demonic darkness to be able to
bear the fiery light of the Holy One. Fire lays waste,   1 Tim. 6:16

bringing death to all the powers of envy and to all that serves death. Fire consumes. The light judges. It brings death to what is dead: dry wood feeds the fire. Death by fire is not caused by rays from the blazing fire but by the nature of death and darkness – opposition to light and enmity to life.

> If eyes are blinded by the sun,
> Blame the eyes, blame not the sun.[3]

Our night-cold nature makes us unable to live in consuming fire. By challenging this cold night, fire breaks in: God's fiery flames are the answer, also, to the call of faith. God descended upon the mountain of Moses in fire. His word is never anything else than fire; his voice flashes flames. Lightning flashes from his heart of burning fire. The Lord on his throne of flaming fire radiates fire from within. He is clothed entirely in flames. His servants and messengers are rays of flame – fire goes out from God. He speaks from the midst of it and his mouth pours forth fire. He sends it down from heaven: devouring fire goes before him. He comes in consuming fire: it is his very nature. He rains down lightning and brimstone. His fury flashes out as fire when his wrath begins. His spirit kindles judgment when he calls for fire. Whoever waits upon God awaits judgment and fire, in which the light of God's salvation shines out.

Exod. 19:18
Ps. 29:7
Dan. 7:9
Deut. 4:36
Ps. 18:8
2 Kings 1:10
Deut. 4:24
Gen. 19:24
Isa. 66:15–16
1 Cor. 3:13

Jesus, our rising sun

Where death and darkness reign, Jesus shines out like the sun after the blackness of tropical night. Paul was blinded when he saw him. Yet he was not to fear the

Matt. 17:2
Acts 9:1–19

---

3 Angelus Silesius (pseudonym for Johannes Scheffler), 1624–1677, *Cherubinischer Wandersmann* (1657).

light forever. After the light had led Paul to become
an apostle of Jesus Christ, he could not remain blind.
In three quiet days of earnest prayer, his inner eye was
opened to the sunlight of the church of Jesus Christ.
Eyes are made for light. Eyes are able to bear light to
the degree that life born of light gains ground. The
surpassing radiance makes them clear and shining. Matt. 6:22

The eagle eye of the Plains Indians and of the
desert Arabs becomes clear and bright in the
shadeless brilliance of their landscape. The more
brightness the eye receives, the more radiance and
light it can bear. Love to God is love for the light. Mic. 7:8–9
God's beauty is radiant glory. Light is his garment. Ps. 104:1–4
Jesus is the light of the world; whoever loves him John 8:12
hungers for his fire. Whoever knows him thirsts for
his light, which outshines all suns. Angelus Silesius
declared, "You may have the light of the sun; my Jesus
is the sun that illuminates my soul."[4]

It is impossible for us to visualize how far the sun
is from the earth it illuminates. Ninety-three million
miles are beyond earthly comprehension. What an
effect this distant kingdom of fiery life has! How
blinding this light is so far from the earth! Against
this distant ball of light, our dazzlingly white mag-
nesium flame appears as black as ink. How can we
grasp it that the light of Rigel is five thousand times
brighter than our sun, or that the rays of Capella send
out in one day as much light as the sun in a hundred
and thirty days!

What effect the proximity of such sun giants must
have is more than we can imagine in human dimen-
sions. In the face of their living energy our little sun
dwindles to a candle. The whole universe, as we see

---

4 Angelus Silesius, *Cherubinischer Wandersmann.*

it in the heavens, is an endless ocean of light made up of many millions of these mighty star-suns. Night is to be found only in the shadow made by the dark planets. If we were able to leave our planet completely behind, we would be exposed to the inconceivable power of a divine sea of light!

In Jesus, a fiery light infinitely stronger than all suns put together draws near to the earth. The footsteps of Jesus come near in burning fire. His eyes are blazing flames. His countenance is radiant with the supreme power of all suns. Seven lampstands of golden fire surround him. Seven sun-stars are in his hand. His light casts man to the ground; the apostle falls at his feet as though dead. The living one, however, gave him the resurrecting power of radiant life: he entrusted to the apostle the glorious mystery of the church, the mystery of the kingdom. Jesus is the rising morning star. It shall become clear to us through the nature of the sun-fire what effect the sevenfold starlight of his church has, what power breaks in with the morning light of the coming day of the sun. The Spirit of Unity is the light of God descending from heaven, closely kin in its inmost nature to the glory of all suns.

Rev. 1:12–17

2 Sam. 23:4

Therefore, if the mission of Jesus is to be understood, the nature of the sun and of fire has to be understood. Our sun is a central fire world from which our planet gets its life. The sun's force of attraction gathers and holds together all the worlds that surround it. Its heat keeps us from dying of cold. Its warmth awakens life in plants and animals. Without its light, all life would perish in darkness. The tiny fraction of light-energy our planet receives from the far distant sun is enough to engender and maintain the boundless life we know on the earth. Every manifestation of earth's power, each breath of wind, the water-vapor cycle, the movements of deep-sea fish, and every beat of our heart is the work of the sun. What bracing power it gives body and soul! Without it we fall prey to death.

We could call every organism on earth a sunbeam come to life. Light and warmth sustain all life. It is the energy of light that makes it possible for plants rooted in the earth to make food from air and earth and to maintain life. Only through light can green plant cells carry out this life-maintaining process. And no living creature, no matter how accustomed to darkness, can live without light or without the organisms belonging to the world of light. The sun is the king and heart of the deep as well as of the heights. The sun is the fire that gives life to all that lives.

It is not by chance that God's being and nature in Christ's radiant glory is compared to the sun, to light, and to fire. What Paul states as a fact – that God's invisible being has been perceptible in his works since the creation of the world – was recognized first and foremost in the light of the sun and in the blaze of fire. Here in the works of creation this eternal power and divine greatness are recognizable with particular force and clarity. From time immemorial, sun and fire have appeared to man as uniquely significant images of divine powers.

Rom. 1:19–20

The first humans worshiped sun and fire

Again and again, God the creator, the spirit of the shining, blazing sun, and the controller of storms and lightning has been worshiped as an all-inclusive oneness. Thus in Egypt the god of the great eternal light was the supreme deity, the creator of all things and the true god of heaven. The light-giving god is the one who reveals and exposes everything. The life-creating god of light is fire that both awakens to life and consumes all that is dead and cold. In India they say of him: "Rays of light proclaim the fire-flashing sun as it rises in splendor to give light to the universe. May the much-to-be desired light of the divine sun awaken our spirit!"[5] The eye of the sun appeared to men of old as supremely beneficent, as the perceptive, good-creating power. "When the sun's eye rises in purity in the east, it spreads its network of light over the sky, the earth, and the firmament, and illuminates everything."[6]

Thus an ancient Brahman prayer says: "Protected by divine power as we gaze at the heavens above the regions of darkness, may we draw near to the deity, to the most radiant light!"[7] In his letter to the Romans, the apostle quite clearly appreciated the pagan recognition of the nature of God; yet at the same time, with the prophets of the Old Testament, he emphasized the other side very strongly, that in those days this shining book of nature was never read outside the ultimate revelation of light in Christ without very dangerous errors being made – without idolatrous misconstructions. Sun and fire were continually being changed from clear and obvious symbols of God's nature to supposedly independent deities of

---

5 Edward Burnett Tylor, *Die Anfänge der Cultur*, vol. 2 (1873).

6 *Rigveda* 1:50, a Hindu hymn to the sun-god Surya.

7 *Rigveda* 1:50.

sun and fire – "lords over all the planet gods" or the dispensers of life itself. The nature of the radiant God of heaven ought to be recognized through his shining creations as infinitely transcending all created things; yet erring humankind all too often exalts the light created by God and makes an idol of it as the highest deity. In this way, unhappy man brings his stifling darkness toward the radiant, created light. When we consider the religious significance of sun and fire, therefore, we must keep pagan idolatry in mind just as much as the dawning intimation of God.

From the earliest times, what was burning and blazing, what was shining and radiant, was seen as divine. In many cultures, the name for God originated from the word that stood for radiant light. God the Father of Heaven was called upon in the old Nordic tongue as "Bright Heaven" in almost the same way as in prophetic truth "the kingdom of heaven" is the kingdom of God. Like the sun, the mighty spirit of the divine light of heaven appears to all people as the life-dispensing and life-sustaining power of the fire of the universe. Through the shining universe, a faint perception of divine unity dawned on fallen man. As a result, he became conscious of the light and unity that alone was to awaken and create the highest form of life. Man implored light and fire to come from heaven. This recognition dawned on the indigenous Americans in the hazy effect of smoke: "Great Spirit, come down and smoke with me as a friend! Fire and earth, smoke with me!"[8]

From the very beginnings of humankind, it was clear to all people, however unenlightened, that

Ps. 136:4–9

---

8 Tylor, *Die Anfänge der Cultur.*

whatever is creative and life-bringing, whatever is good and noble, has radiant warmth and blazing brightness. Down through the ages, people have always been conscious that the warmth of light and love's life and vitality belong together. Light and beauty are one. But light does not shine everywhere. The sun goes down. Night follows day. Throughout the ages people have always known that the radiant, blazing brightness of the good and powerful spirit of light has an opposite – the evil, sinister spirit of cold and darkness. Everything that is tarnished and ugly, that prevents enlightenment and knowledge, and that threatens and kills life is freezing, unredeemed darkness, filled with hidden dangers. Everything that opposes day is night. Everything that keeps back the awakening life of spring is winter's death. Everything that opposes warmth is deadening cold. Everything that opposes unifying love causes disintegration and death. Death threatens life. Between light and darkness there is enmity and warfare to the end.

Man is placed in a tremendous tension between life and death: he is called to burning, life-giving light, but can he overcome or conquer the freezing cold and deadly darkness? Will he survive in the struggle against this very dangerous power, which constantly besets him from within and without? The good spirit of light was revealed from the very beginning as divine, as the leader and champion of life. The evil spirit of darkness was from the very beginning the enemy, the sinister demon of night and death. Between the two stood man, struggling as it were between heaven and hell. This struggle filled his life. Full of alarm, he feared descending night as the

Eccles. 11:7–8

cold threat of death and hell. Rejoicing, he greeted the
dawn of shining day as the approach of the glowing
warmth of the heavens and of life.

For man, light was life and power. He saw the
morning sun rise glorious to course triumphant
across the heavens. In the sun, in light, and in fire,   Ps. 19:1–7
he saw nothing soft or insipid, nothing weak or
servile. In his eyes, the victorious power of light was
armed with the radiant arrows of the sun and the
flashing weapon of lightning. In his eyes, the strong
sun-hero of radiant morning and of bright springtime
was welded in a fiery unity with the thunder-god of
storms and threatening lightning. The light-god of
the sun's power was for him masculine and manly,
like the thunder-god of storms and lightning. Spring,
when the sun is ascending, was for him a youthful,
courageous war hero, who as a triumphant con-
queror overcomes the aging giant of mighty winter
and leads in a new time over the earth and all its
inhabitants – the sunny time, the longed-for time, the
expected time! This time alone can awaken strong,
prolific, and abiding life.

Light was to triumph over darkness at the end of   Rev. 21:22–25
time. The day was to dawn when the last springtime   Rev. 22:5
of all worlds and ages would melt and abolish forever
the whole present age of wintertime – this cold, dark,
dead, and numbing ice age of the world of today.
In early Christian times, Hermas, a prophet of the
church of Rome, wrote his book *The Shepherd,*
in which this age-old enlightenment is given new
meaning in the early Christian sense. In the third
and fourth parables he says, "The present age is
wintertime. . . . The age to come is summertime."

What facts lie behind this prophetic language? It is important to get a picture of what sun and fire are and have meant in nature from time immemorial if we want to understand all the prophetic Word has to say about the sun-energy of God, about the light of Christ, about the fire of the Spirit, about the dawn of radiant day in the coming kingdom, and about the living church with its fire of unity and its power to shine forth.

Ps. 84:11

Isa. 9:2

Matt. 3:11

People learned to master fire

Nothing can make the powerful significance of glowing fire clearer to us than the very beginnings of humankind when man, cast out of the garden and still far from God, met fire for the first time. It came as a terror to humankind. And yet the same fire was soon kindled as a campfire and as a sacrificial altar fire! Adam was once master over fire, and light shone in him. But what happened after this light was lost? How did the first man, cast out into the darkness, experience fire? In a flash, lightning would descend from heaven with a crack of thunder, and a forest giant would be set ablaze. Everything would take flight. Soon, however, people would gather round the felled and still burning tree, encamp there to feed the fire as their own, and so find protection for the community they craved.

Lev. 6:12–13

Or it could be that the depths of the mountain would rumble. The foundations of the earth would quake and crack. Enormous pillars of fire would shoot up out of the smoking mountain. Volleys of stones and showers of ashes would be hurled high into the air and immediately spread far and wide over the

land. Slowly a river of glowing, blood-red substance
would pour its way into the valley. Trees or bushes
would be caught by its fiery breath, and everything
would go up in flames! Gradually the surface of the
red-hot lava would grow pale. It would lie there like
a gigantic snake, covering the valley bed in a mound
of heat. Man would venture to draw his camp nearer
the slowly hardening lava. The nearer he came, the
warmer he would be, even in the middle of the cold
tropical night. Should a piece of dry wood touch this
dangerous glowing stream, the branch would burst
into bright flames. Then fire would be kindled, just
as when the tree was struck by lightning. And as man
put more and more wood on the fire, the warmer and
brighter would the flames become.

So man learned to combine his terrible fear of fire
with a reverent thankfulness, for here he encountered
an element that united the wrath of a destructive
power with the loving gift of life. In reverence man
wanted to preserve it, so he fed and tended it. He
learned how to acquire and handle it. Soon he began
to carry it, glowing and glimmering, to kindle a
blazing fire where he wanted it, using tiny sticks. He
carefully kept alive the glowing embers borrowed
from the destructive lightning or volcano, carrying
them to where it was cold and dark. He learned to
take care of the fire.

So man revered the spark of fire as something
sacred, a truly holy possession the deity had given
to the human race alone. No animal had an active
part in this possession or took it along. No gathering of animals tended the fire as humans did. Only
the frail human community was never without fire;

Exod. 20:18–25

only humans were fire bearers. The spark was never allowed to go out in their hands. "Fire guardian" was man's name. He must never forget his fire. He passed it on from hand to hand. True to his origin and his goal, man as fire giver and fire borrower proved to be a communal being. Fire united people in mutual help. Even the total stranger was included in this fellowship from the very beginning.

Fire gathered people in community

Tending the fire was basic for human community. The radiation of light and warmth generated a power to gather. The campfire meant that community was formed and preserved. The most valuable heritage of the people of old was the community fire passed on from generation to generation. Everywhere, the flame remains the focal point of all human cravings for community. It is the flame that brings about community as a way of life. The first light of God's image was lost when humankind fell. A sign of the new humankind was that it fostered the flames originating from those terrors of the heavens and of the abyss. Then, after the loss of God's first peace, it dawned on man that judgment by fire meant a gift of fire, that the wrath of the highest powers bears within it new, loving grace. Service to the fire became service to God; man, worshiping the God whom he had lost, wanted to keep the warm glow of the fire alive through the sacrifice of wood. He did not want its light to go out at any time. His aim was to gather the community and to keep it gathered. Food also, like life, should be preserved from decay and death. Thus the community of the tribe, of the nation, and of humankind was meant to come into being from

Luke 3:16–17

Ps. 29:7

campfire, hearth fire, and altar fire. The light of
paradise had disappeared, unclouded community
with God had been lost. Could the new communal
fire light the way back to God?

Through fire, man very slowly gained more
mastery over the forces of nature – the mastery he
had been called to in the lost garden. People seemed
to become more and more free, especially in choosing
and changing their habitation. They felt increasingly
independent of the outward circumstances of country
and climate. In the community of the fire, they strove
to press forward to the freedom and mastery they
had forfeited along with God's community of light.
A glowing light once more gathered them round a
blazing central point. It showed them a communal
way through the threatening night to where freedom
prevailed. It seemed to them that the brightness of
the flame would set them free from the cold's deadly
breath and from all the forces of nature that tried to
tear them to pieces and destroy them once they had
lost the peace of God.

Set free from the fear of night and from
enslavement to nature, if only to a small extent, man
could venture slowly to take up his lost mastery over
things and circumstances. So people learned to share
their food in community; they learned how to keep
it edible for the whole band. So they made a step
forward from the campfire in the open, on the bare
ground, to the protected community hearth made of
two layers of stone set opposite each other, between
which the holy fire was to burn uninterruptedly
for all. Here it was to be kept alive for the tribe for
always, an awe-inspiring mystery of the hoped-for
community.

Isa. 10:16–18

Fear and terror had once led to a common flight from the unpredictable fiery wrath of the deity; later, a common reverence bound people to the flame. For they had experienced what the dangerous fire gave the tribe: protection from freezing to death and from the evil powers of night, conservation of life-energies and preservation of food by seasoning with fire. But fire's power to gather people was seen more and more as its most powerful element. The much-desired gift of life and community was greater than the destruction caused by lightning and fire-belching mountains that had once driven people apart. What had once meant the terror of death and separation became a power for life, a power that gathered.

This is how humans tried to survive the awful horror of the Ice Age. This is how they passed through those deadly ages that drove much mightier animal species into distant parts or completely exterminated them. Only thus could humans, lacking claws and sharp teeth, hold their own against the countless murderous creatures of night. Only thus could their heart withstand the spirits of darkness, whom they feared most of all.

The home evolved to protect the flame

The fire gave protection; for this reason it was protected. As the protective gathering point of the community, it became the focal point of the human dwelling. Houses were created for the sake of the fire. People first started to build houses in an effort to protect the flame. The sacred hearth fire is not without reason the very essence of home life. In choosing a campsite, the only consideration was to protect the flame, to find a shield for the hearth, not to find or erect a sheltered hiding place. Once protected from the wind, the blazing flames frightened away all the dangers that threatened, whereas no hiding place, however carefully chosen, could hold off stealthy and evil powers.

To shelter the fireplace from storms and floods, walls were set up under the cover of trees, or sometimes the fireplace was built in a protecting cave. But in each case the shelter afforded by the embryonic house was mainly for keeping the flame alive. Not the house but the fire was protection from freezing to death in the ice-cold night and from being frightened by nocturnal enemies. It was not themselves but the fire that people tried to protect with walls and roof. Its protection was a holy cause, the holiest obligation. The dwelling house evolved as a sacred shelter for the hearth.

Therefore the same name – fireplace – is used for this house (whose life-giving central point always was and will be the flame) and for the temple (in whose Holy of Holies the fire burns).[9] The open camping place of nomadic tribes had become a home through the bright burning of a fire. Then the house evolved around the flame that needed constant guarding. The wind-shelter (which was not to protect hardened humans but the fire) became the place of the fire, the protective home for the cherished flame. And later, as the wind-shelter became a roofed hut, the hearth fire was still the decisive factor in human habitations. At first the fire was laid on the bare ground. Gradually a heap of stones was piled up, becoming a raised hearth, the important center of the dwelling.

---

9 For example, the Latin *aedes* (house, temple) derives from the Proto-Indo-European *eidh* (to burn).

The hearth became a holy place

The raised hearth was the token of a holy place, symbolizing the great cause that held people together. It became a holy symbol of sublime significance, an altar and a memorial. The word "altar" was used for God's holy, blazing hearth of smoking sacrifice in the temple, and the same word was used for the cooking fireplace in every secular house – this was holy too. For primitive people, the hearth of their daily dwelling was just as inviolable as the altar fire in a temple. The reason is clear. Light and warmth, as gifts of the deity, were always the power that gathered the community. Since the very first human community, the hearth needed reverent care as the crystallization point of the common life.

The raised fireplace was a symbol of great significance not only for the living community but also for the dead. In the earliest times of communal life, communities constantly moved from place to place, and, with the passage of time, the old leaders of the tribe passed away one by one. Along the path taken by the tribe, holy symbols arose as abiding memorials and permanently sacred places. Wherever the holy community fires had burned, wherever a gathering ground had been a place of sacrifice and religious union, earth and stones would be piled up to make a mound, which kept on getting higher and wider. The first memorials made by man were marks of old fireplaces consecrated to the eternal.

They were rightly regarded as holy graves by those who traveled past. Tombs of primitive people, especially of those who had played a leading role, were erected beside their beloved hearths where they had

lived and worked in the midst of their people. There
the dead should receive the honors due to them. Just
as the altar of a temple and the hearth of a simple
house were given the same veneration, the tomb and
the hearth also became one at this same fire. The
tomb became a place that was consecrated forever:
the former fireplace, beside which the dead person
had been active in life, was preserved as a holy place
by enclosing the hearth and the grave within a circle
of stones. Thus arose the "hill of worship" where
God and heathen gods were worshiped, as it says in
the Bible.

1 Sam. 10:5

Deut. 12:2–3

With the living, it was the same as with the dead.
The area around the fire was enclosed more and more
until a closed square was created, housing the living
in the same way as the stone circle housed the dead.
The vital center for the living as for the dead was and
always will be the home hearth, the holy hearth – the
very essence of the home and of family life. The
words for fence (*Zaun* in German), town (*tun* in Old
English), enclosure (*tún* in Old Norse), and fortress
(*dún* in Old Irish), with their common Nordic root,
point to the fire and the buildings around it. Around
the fire, the permanent center, arose the individual
house, providing a roof for the hearth. And around
this hearth the settlement grew up, its fences and
walls protecting the roofed dwellings: the fire is the
secret at the heart of all communal dwelling.

Fire as a token of peace and unity

The hearth fire, then, was regarded as the power
uniting the communal household settled around
it, just as earlier (as a campfire) it had gathered the

Isa. 4:5 nomadic tribe. And despite a tendency in all people to limit their community to their own kin, the fire would stimulate friendship between tribes. The fire, as the basis of hospitality, would pave the way for peace and unity between strangers, and by freely borrowing and lending the fire, even enemy tribes became friendly. Carried from hearth to hearth and from one people to another, fire would be given or received as a token of peace and unity.

The first symbol of peace and the first gift of hospitality was the smoldering spark of fire, the sign of community in the tribe. Again, the service paid to the dead indicates to posterity the friendly relationships between the living. The community of food, field, and fire among these primitive people becomes clear in their service to the dead. The dead were provided with food and fire in their graves, just as in life they had practiced community of food and fire with the living. Primitive people helped each other in community of goods and communal life; the fields and pastures consecrated by fire were under the communal management of the whole tribe or village. The dead, too, like every other member of the tribe, had to be provided with the earthly goods of the community. They were not to be left cold and hungry in a dark grave. Therefore they were given a share of the communal food or the harvest from a piece of land that was dedicated to them. But the fire surrendered to the dead was a bigger sacrifice than the food. Nothing that belonged by rights to the dead was to be kept back for the living.

From ancient times, therefore, when a man died, the fire he had shared to the last in living community was extinguished; it was to be surrendered to him completely as a consecrated gift. As a result, after the fire had been put out on the deserted hearth, a completely new fire had to be kindled. Still today, the Roman Catholic Church extinguishes all the old fires on Easter Saturday to commemorate Jesus' death and lights the new flames on Easter morning so that every household can light its Easter fires or its Easter candles from it. Primitive people, in giving fire, testi- Luke 12:49 fied to their faith that life continued for the dead. Today, too, as the candles are relighted, the cry rings out: "Christ is risen!"

Because of their faith in life after death, primitive people gave to the dead what they held to be the best and the highest also for the living. As the dead were given food and fire for a new and different life, the living were given food and fire for every new under-taking on earth. Fire-bearing "fire-virgins" were indispensable as an escort for every move or new beginning. Roman youths consecrated to the found-ing of a new settlement were sent out from the parent stock on the first of March. So, too, were Germanic youths, the "sacred spring" dedicated to the deity. As the consecrated "spring" of the race, they had to take the community fire with them when they were ready to leave, while all home fires were extinguished. The holy tending of the fire and the kindling of the new spark were entrusted to the fire-virgins, who were not to be hindered in this priestly service by love of men or by childbearing. Later, chastity was still rigorously demanded of the Vestal Virgins[10] too, and of the consecrated virgins who watched the holy temple fire.

---

10 In ancient Rome, these priestesses of Vesta, goddess of the hearth, tended a sacred flame on which the security of the city depended.

Lev. 6:9–13

The continued protection and maintenance of the tribe settled on home ground also depended on service to the holy fire. Continuance of the race and continuance of the fire were regarded as one and the same thing. When the tribe died out, the fire went out; as soon as the fire ceased to burn, the independence of the people was lost. And should a traveling band lose its flame, they would fetch a new spark from the old home hearth, so as not to be indebted to strangers. Thus Grettir the Strong swam through the stormy waves of the fjord and brought fire back in his uplifted hand.[11] As Homer says in *The Odyssey*, "The seed of fire is fostered, that it need not be kindled afar."[12]

Through fire, the homeland was dedicated to the tribe and its deity. Just as the flame of the land was held in holy community, so from time immemorial the land, as "common land," was common property with no individual possession – marked-out land held communally by the "commonalty." For the Norwegians, "to sanctify with fire" meant taking over territory with their communal flame. Where their fires burned was their homeland. The home fire, like the land they had taken over, belonged to the whole community of the tribe.

Like possessing the land in common, sharing the tribe's fire was a religious matter. To be denied fire meant banishment from the homeland. Fire could be refused only to one exiled for religious reasons, only as a punitive measure sanctioned by divine power – as a ban. Left to be judged by the gods, exiles could no longer share the necessities of life with their

11 *The Saga of Grettir the Strong*, chapter 39, fourteenth-century Icelandic.

12 Homer, *The Odyssey*, 5.490.

people; the fire they requested was denied them, their homeland forbidden.

Therefore, to be exiled, this hardest fate that could befall anyone, was called "being deprived of the community of water and fire." As Herodotus reports about Aristodemus of Sparta, if fire was not given to a man no one spoke to him.[13] Similarly, according to Cornelian law, loss of Roman citizenship was pronounced by denying a person water and fire. Among Germanic peoples also, no one was allowed to give outlaws fire or water; they were cut off from the whole communal life of the people.

This granting or refusing of fire had a leveling effect. With regard to women, the flame had an elevating effect, raising them to a status of equality or even to priestly dignity. All people are equal before the fire. Women everywhere had the greatest importance in giving or withholding this holy service, as with the Vestal Virgins or the fire-bearing virgins of the Vikings and other Germanic peoples, who were consecrated to the service of sacred springtime. It was nearly always the woman who had to tend the hearth fire, guard and foster it, carry it with her, and feed it with ever-ready material.

The swastika, a co-opted symbol

Perhaps woman was also the first to bring fire to birth by rubbing sticks, for it was in the process of work that the way to rekindle the lost flame was discovered. In the process of making tools or cutting wood to feed the fire, a new spark would fall into the pile of wood dust and blaze up into a precious flame,

---

13 Herodotus, c. 484–c. 425 BC, *The Histories* 7.231.

the result of heat and friction and the collection of fine particles of wood. Work with fire-making materials was a holy function – a priestly service. Fire was generated by rapidly twirling two sticks (called the fire-father and fire-mother), so that, as the *Edda* says, "it could be allowed to grow and immediately send messages far and wide."[14] This kindling of fire, practiced by men or women, was from the very beginning a sacred service. Among the American Indians, the priest was called the "fire maker" just as the priestesses of Rome were called the "fire-virgins."

The swastika (symbolizing both a wheel of fire and the turning wheel of the sun) points to this kindling of flame, which from remotest times was held to be holy. The swastika is an ancient symbol of fire sticks laid at right angles. The hooks at the ends of the sticks suggest quick motion like a whirling wheel, showing the quick rotation that causes ignition. The spark is the result of the motion. Thus in the Far East the swastika, as the fire-cross denoting kindling in primitive times, became the symbol for cause and effect. Rotary friction was recognized as the cause and fire as the effect – obviously with insight into the effect of sin, the karma of evil, a first recognition of this significant law.

The fact that we find this fire-cross of two hooked sticks as early as the New Stone Age proves that it had universal significance. As a symbol of life and community, the kindling of fire by the twirling of sticks is the common property of all peoples. As a symbol of fire-kindling and of the sun-wheel, the swastika belongs to primeval man. All his descendants,

---

14 The *Edda*, a thirteenth-century collection of Icelandic poems and prose.

without distinction of race or blood, have a right to it. So it is not surprising that all the Aryan tribes as well as the Phoenicians of Canaan preserved this sign of the life-giving power of sunlight and fire-kindling. Fire, the kindling of fire, and the community of fire belong also to the Jewish inhabitants of Canaan.

The fire of burnt offering

Among early peoples, the holy service of guarding and kindling the consuming fire led to sacrifice by fire on the holy altar. So the people of Israel worshiped Yahweh-Jehovah every morning and evening through the ascending smoke of the incense offering and the rising flames of the burnt offering. Offerings on the incense altar become in the new covenant the fiery offering of intercession: Jesus Christ, the high priest, interceding for his people. At the same time, through the pleading of Jesus and the Holy Spirit, they are the fiery prayers rising from his saints, also described as daily offerings.

Exod. 30:1

Heb. 5:1–3
Heb. 9:1–14

Rev. 5:8

The burnt offering on the fire-altar, Israel's whole offering, was not only the most frequent but also the most common and comprehensive sacrifice, the complete sacrifice. Abraham, for instance, the patriarch of Israel, showed an unlimited readiness to sacrifice when he was prepared to give the only son of the promise as a sacrifice by fire. And even before the patriarchs, Noah, saved from the annihilating flood, sent up to heaven and to God's rainbow of peace a burnt offering of a whole animal, a symbol of complete dedication. For this reason, Paul spoke of the death of Jesus as the fire offering of the new covenant, of his cross-gallows as the altar of burnt offering.

Lev. 1

Gen. 22

Gen. 8:9, 20
Heb. 13:11–12
Eph. 5:2

But John saw and heard those who had witnessed to Christ with their blood – saw them under the altar, like the spirits of the men of old under the hearth that was their grave and their memorial. In this baptism of blood, Jesus' question was answered: "Can you be baptized with the same fire that comes over me?" The blood baptism of the Crucified One and the church's martyrdom by death afterward point to the complete sacrifice, as if on the hearth of a burnt offering.

Among the people of Israel, the flame of a sacrifice that pointed in such a way to the ultimate could be kindled only at the holy altar fire. No "alien" fire was allowed on the altar. As among the most ancient peoples, the fire blazing on Israel's table of burnt offering was never to die out. As eternal fire, it was sanctified to God. The stone hearth or stone table (which even at this time was occasionally built up with earth and turf) was later, at the time of the prophets, called "God's mountain" or "God's hearth." As the table for the fire, it was the altar of God.

In accordance with age-old custom, this altar, the place of sacrifice and fire, was built of undressed stone even as late as the second temple of Israel. Moses (like very early peoples) made a fire-altar of earth and surrounded it with twelve piles of stone as the Israelites' court of sanctuary; Joshua (like later primitive peoples) made one of undressed stone and surrounded it with the stones of the Law. In the new covenant, commitment unto death must be offered, as it were, on just such an ancient burnt-offering altar as Abel's, without the artificial embellishment of human skill and its sham riches, in the primal simplicity of humanity at its poorest and simplest.

Rev. 6:9–11

Mark 10:38–40

Matt. 20:22

Exod. 29

Ezek. 43:12–15

Deut. 27:5–6

Exod. 20:24–25

Josh. 8:30–31

When the apostles of Jesus proclaim him who was baptized by fire and executed on a crude cross, their words have effect only if they have no rhetorical skill or lofty wisdom. Sacrifice by fire demands utmost simplicity – the original genuineness.

1 Cor. 1:17

To sum up, it was by that simple fire-altar in the temple court that the prophet Isaiah recognized the full significance of the fire of God: "God has a hearth in Jerusalem." "Yahweh has a fire in Zion." "Jehovah will kindle a light-giving fire over all the dwellings on his mountain so that in burning it may shine through the dark night!" "The light of Israel will be fire." "His Spirit will judge and will kindle a fire."

Isa. 31:9

Isa. 4:4–5

Isa. 10:17

Isa. 66:15–16

God appears as fire

Like lightning from heaven, the fire of the Lord comes down to strike where it will. When Elijah, the only remaining prophet of Jehovah, confronted hundreds of false prophets who represented the sun-god Baal and the moon-and-Venus goddess Astarte, he ordered two altars to be prepared, one for the idols and the other for Yahweh, the God of Abraham, Isaac, and Israel. He built his of twelve stones because it stood like Moses' for the hearth of the twelve tribes, Jehovah's people. He poured water over it; for on both altars, wood and a beast of sacrifice were to be laid, but no fire of human making. The priests of Baal and Astarte were to call on their gods, and Elijah was to call on his God to send lightning to kindle fire: "The god who answers with fire, he is God!"

1 Kings 18

1 Kings 18:24

Here the battle between the fire-gods and the fire coming from God was settled. The frantic calling of the priests of sun and moon got no response. When

Elijah called, however, the fire of Jehovah fell from heaven upon his altar and devoured burnt offering, wood, stone, earth, and even water, the enemy of fire; the flash of lightning proved that "Jehovah is God.

1 Kings 18:39 Yahweh is God. The Lord is God!"

Fire that descends from heaven is the blazing sign in which the God of the covenant draws near. For he is the creative spirit of the central fire; he created heaven and earth, sun, light, glowing heat, and all

Isa. 33:14 life. Consuming fire proclaims God's approach. When Abraham, the patriarch of divine faith, asked for a sign of the covenant to put all his doubts aside, it was God's flame of fire that came between the pieces of the sacrifice at the right and the left, just as people making a covenant used to stride between the

Gen. 15:8–18 parts of the divided animal to strengthen their vow. God makes his covenant with fire; this covenant we must follow.

When the dwelling place of the covenant – the tabernacle – was set up in the wilderness, a shining flame and a cloud of smoke settled over it because it was the house of God's fire. When this fire of God would not move ahead, the people stayed at their camping

Num. 9:15–22 place and waited, even for months at a time! When the flame went ahead with a cloud of smoke, however, the whole company, pledged to the fire, made its departure. They saw the guiding light of the fire as God's call, God's breath, and God's word. God, the sender of fire, was himself their fire bearer, and it was impossible to make any move unless he went ahead.

Again, to give the prophet Moses his commission, God appeared to him as flames of fire in a burning

Exod. 3:2–10 bush. God's word was a burning fire also to Jeremiah;

it glowed in his heart and became a blazing flame in
his mouth. This is also said of Elijah; he burst forth
with his prophecy like a burning fire. Fire and smoke
are signs of God that break in like flaming words
to proclaim his glory – both as the fire of wrath and
judgment and as the fire of love and unity.

Jer. 5:14

Joel 2:30

2 Sam. 22:9

Ps. 18:8

The fire of God's judgment

The fire of God's light never appears without the
judgment that consumes what is old, what is withered and dried up, what is lifeless, disunited, and
unjust – all that has fallen prey to death. Humankind
should never forget that fire from heaven and from
the abyss came to man in lightning and in volcanic
eruption. Bringing fear and terror, it strikes into the
cold darkness of night and unpeace. It floods the dead
and withered landscape with a fiery sea of horror. It
reveals and consumes the darkness of evil, death, and
separation. Always, the fire of judgment must burn
the felled tree and the useless chaff.

Heb. 12:29

Matt. 7:19

Matt. 3:12

God calls down this fire as a final judgment
over the darkened universe, just as he let it fall on
impure and degenerate Sodom and Gomorrah, on
the tyrannical injustice of Egypt with its slavery, and
on the divisive and rebellious company of Korah and
other subversive Israelites in the wilderness. It will
consume heaven and earth. Like jewels to be tried by
fire, they are destined for a sea of flame, kindled on
the day of the last judgment that destroys all that is
divided and separated from God.

Gen. 19:24

Exod. 9:23–24

Num. 16:31–35

2 Pet. 3:7, 10

Rev. 21:8

In this judgment, a grim, dark fire will be kindled,
sending out jets of torturing smoke without the blessing of justifying flames. The hellish fire of expulsion

and banishment is the last mystery of judgment. It is separated from all community of life, from all the protecting and liberating power of the camp or hearth fire. It burns with lurid flames and belongs to the nocturnal powers of darkness. In the Sermon on the Mount Jesus declares that whoever destroys the community of love and despises his brother and denies him dignity, whoever leaves the hungry and thirsty without food and drink or the homeless and naked without shelter and clothes, whoever ignores the sick and imprisoned deserves this final fire of judgment because he has forgotten God and love.

Matt. 5:22
Matt. 25:41–46

Cold hearts that shut out the misery of others, that are callous to injustice, and that resist community in their hardheartedness call down judgment upon themselves – they are cast out into the consuming darkness of complete absence of community because their whole nature has the characteristics of darkness. Jesus declares this very severe judgment inescapable: divisive, destructive, and disintegrating unpeace must be exposed and judged. There is no other way of approaching this unpeace. Yet Jesus, in proclaiming impending judgment, wants to bring salvation. His fire judges evil by showing the way out of the dominion of darkness into the kingdom of light. In his hand, the torch of wrath becomes the dispenser of gathering and sustaining life.

Jesus, bringer of God's fire

Jesus is God's fire-bringer. The early Christians preserved this memorable saying of Jesus: "He who is near me is near the fire; he who is far from me is

far from the kingdom."[15] Jesus glows like fire and sun;
he brings the judgment of the Spirit of Fire; through
the approach of his kingdom of light, he lays the
foundation of the community of fire in his church
household. With him comes God's kingdom, God's
rulership; God himself is the shining sun, putting
all created suns in the shade forever. In the light and
unity of Jesus Christ, God's heart of glowing, blazing
love has achieved the fulfillment of his eternal will.
The Son is the sun hero, who needs no created suns
when he brings in the victory of the coming age of
light. His radiance is consuming fire and life-creating
light. "Just as the sun fills all substance that absorbs
its strength, so the voice of God echoes through all
people – but also as a voice of wrath. If a plant has no
sap, the sun's rays burn it; but if it does have sap, the
sun's rays warm it and make it grow."[16] If we are not
ready for God's fire of love, for Jesus Christ's victory
of light, we succumb to the fury of the all-consuming
judgment of fire.

In the burning love of Christ's approach, the
blazing wrath of judgment by fire comes to an end.
Annihilation ceases in his glowing warmth; life
begins in his Spirit of Light. His followers know
that, unlike Elijah, they cannot intervene and call
down destructive fire on the enemies of the cause,
or actually spew it forth themselves. They know how
loving is the Spirit whose children they are. As when
Elijah ascended, their fire, coming from God's radiant
heart, is seen in the sun-chariot and the horses of

Marginal references:
Luke 17:24
Rev. 21:23
Rev. 22:5
Luke 12:49
2 Kings 1:10–15
Luke 9:54–55

---

15 Quoted by Origen, *Homily on Jeremiah*, XX.3.

16 Jakob Böhme, 1575–1624, quoted in Alfred Wiesenhütter, *Morgenröte: Jakob Böhme in einer Auswahl aus seinen sämtlichen Schriften* (Eberhard Arnold Verlag, 1925), 182–183.

fire that carry the liberated spirits of all nations into

2 Kings 2:11 God's unifying kingdom of light. The burning fire of Christ's followers shows itself in their fiery mission of love, in the glowing light of their joyful message. Their nature is that of messengers sent out by God: through their service the light of the heavenly world is brought to those who are to inherit the salvation of the final kingdom.

The mission of Jesus Christ brings the Holy Spirit as the radiant, burning spirit of perfect love. The fire of this mission, originating in the coming world of light, consumes all that is unholy and fans to radiant brightness all that is of God. Jesus came to kindle a sea of fire on the earth. His whole longing is for it to burn. He is the last of the men of old, one who has never fallen. As the bearer of the Spirit of Fire, he is the only possible bearer of the light, guardian of the embers, and kindler of the fire. His flame of the Spirit offers us our last chance of becoming true men and women, of uniting with God, and of being brothers and sisters in community.

The first Adam forfeited the privileges of his holy calling: the old nature spurned the possibility of the life of light once granted it. But God did not want people to lose forever their destiny of light as his image. He sent to earth the divine flame and loving fire of the last Adam, and in him the burning light of God breaks in again. In its white-hot glow lives the strength to awaken life, the light- and life-bestowing

1 Cor. 15:22, 45 energy of the new creation.

Through the blazing flame of the Spirit of Jesus Christ, people once enslaved by fear of death are set

Heb. 2:15 free from all bestial and infernal powers of night so that from now on they can assume lordship of spirit over the aging powers of nature and also over their own bodies and souls, both creatures of the first creation. Only the power of the Holy Spirit of Jesus Christ can bring about kingly freedom. For only he who is more powerful than any other spirit is able to bring the authority and lordship of the Father of Jesus Christ to victory over the enslaving powers of death.

The flame of the Spirit gathers God's people
The power to gather and protect, coming from the flame of the Spirit, drives away the murderous spirits of night; it supplants the ice age of the prevailing world-spirit, which causes everything to grow cold; but not only that – it brings, with its blazing protection, the one thing that is decisive for our world and age: the church gathered round the altar fire of the Crucified One, the communal household of God with its missionary bands sent out into all the world.   Acts 2–4

The focal point of this new people is the new fireplace of the new church; around it a communal settlement arises once more. Around the radiant fire of the Holy Spirit, the spiritual temple is built up as a tangible house of God: the city on the hill, whose   Eph. 2:18–22
light streams out over all lands. Her place of worship   Matt. 5:14
is on fire with the Spirit; she shines forth in the truth. The fire of the Holy Spirit brings the church   John 4:23–24
above – the glorified ones who have witnessed with their blood – down to the band of believers gathered round Christ's throne of fire. In this flame of the   1 Thess. 4:13–18
Spirit, there is living unity between those who have gone before and those who remain on earth. The unanimity of the people gathered to full community

in the house of God is the unity of the church above

Heb. 12:22–23 that dwells in perfect light, inaccessible to the mortal life of our darkened earth.

From the city above, the fire of love descends and takes the leadership. Coming from the Spirit of perfect unity, it leads the body of believers in all its weakness not only to community of goods – food, land, and everything else – and to community of work: it leads them to pass on this flame through hospitality and fiery mission, serving as messengers to all people on earth. From the kingdom of light, the unity of the church becomes a message of peace for the whole world.

For this fire-carrying service, the holy flame of the church's pure Spirit must be kept unadulterated. The church of fire can maintain permanence only because she fosters and reveres the holy flame to the end. Those united in faith and love in the church protect not themselves but the flame of the Spirit, the only surety of true life. What they try to preserve is not their own lives but that of the holy fire, to which they have surrendered their own nature. Only in this way do they gain real life, which shall become full-

Matt. 10:39 ness of life for everyone. Their hearth burns for the whole world without assimilating the unholy fires of other elements from the world. Nothing of man's own nature, no alien fire from other altars, no other spirit

1 Cor. 3:16–17 may approach. The church's altar of light is holy; her works of love are of a different nature from man's.

Yet as soon as her radiant fire is mixed with the fuel of alien flames, it dies out. When such a church community forgets the light of unadulterated love and denies its first works, which were free from everything alien to love, its lampstand is knocked

over and its light goes out. As soon as the inviolable   Rev. 2:5
fire of the Holy Spirit is taken from such a community, it loses its commission and its freedom.
The dying hearth ceases to be an altar; robbed of
the fire of God's love, it is nothing but worthless
ashes. Without light, the house of this people is no
longer a temple of God. Unity and community are
extinguished with the loss of fire; they have become
impossible. The church can never gather without the
focal point of holy light and fire. Only when the holy
flame of the Spirit is called down from its homeland
in the church above, can such a lost people be set
free again from the dominion of slavery and lack of
community.

Without the fire of the Holy Spirit, community
dies. It peters out in slavery to alien peoples where
other flames burn – unholy fires of man's own works
and the emotional enthusiasm of blood, which is
demonic! The land once consecrated to common
use through the divine fire of the Spirit now belongs
once again (with all the work done on it and with all
it produces) to self-interest or group egoism, whereas
in the church it had at long, long last belonged to
God! In the church of Christ was realized in a small,
hidden way what will appear in greatness at the end
of time: "The earth is the Lord's!" It belongs to God.   Ps. 24:1
No inch of its land may be claimed as the property of
an individual. Where the Spirit of the last and eternal
king rules, the land belongs to the light and fire of his
church and his kingdom. Where God's flame goes
out, God is robbed of his land, and it falls back to
private property. The life of community is dead.

Yet the message of the gospel is resurrection from
the dead. From his resurrection on, Christ shows

Luke 24:46–49

himself as the Son of God in the coming down of the Holy Spirit again and again. When the old flame has gone out – when the living, as slaves to death, drift apart and turn away from the hearth that once gathered them, and leave it to those men of old (now dead and gone) who were faithful to their altar – then the Spirit of the Risen One wants to kindle new fire to set up community of life again with the watchword: "Light your lamps! The Lord is truly risen!"

An expectant church awaits the bridegroom
Inspired by the Easter message and the Pentecostal flame of the Holy Spirit, young people – "the holy springtime" – set out to consecrate new land to the church of the Risen One. Again and again, bands of awakened young people have set out. A hundred years after the first full community in Jerusalem, a new outpouring of the Spirit of Fire created the church anew in Asia Minor. In total community, this church awaited the Jerusalem that was to come down from God, the image of God's city-state, the work of God alone. With mutual hospitality, they waited for this city with its holy order of divine justice. In the suspense of this expectation, virgins carrying fire appeared before the gathering of believers and wept in repentance, as if bewailing the dead, and lamented over the life people were leading, estranged from God.[17] As a result of the gospel thus proclaimed with power characteristic of the future, a life took shape that corresponded to the coming kingdom. The serving church was to learn how to direct the holy life in such a way that the purifying fire of God's

17 Epiphanius, *Panarion*, 49.2.

future might bring the all-embracing harmony of true community.

More than a hundred years after that, Methodius the Martyr sang of these fire-virgins of the expectant church:

> From on high, O virgins,
> Rang out the voice that quickeneth the dead,
> "Go out in haste to meet the bridegroom,
> Robed in white and bearing lamps,
> Before the morning dawns. Awake,
> Before the Lord doth vanish through the door!"
> I consecrate myself to thee,
> And bearing lamps that shed forth light,
> I go to meet thee, bridegroom.
>
> O Christ, thou art the prince of life.
> All hail, thou light that never settest!
> Hear our cry!
> The choir of virgins calleth to thee,
> Thou flower of life, thou love itself,
> Joy, understanding, wisdom, everlasting word!
> I consecrate myself to thee,
> And bearing lamps that shed forth light,
> I go to meet thee, bridegroom.
>
> No longer is man robbed of paradise,
> For thou dost give once more by thy decree
> The land he lost
> Through guile of cunning serpent,
> O immortal, unshakable, blessed one!
> I consecrate myself to thee,
> And bearing lamps that shed forth light,
> I go to meet thee, bridegroom.[18]

---

18 Saint Methodius of Olympus, *Banquet of the Ten Virgins*, Discourse 11, chapter 2 (abridged).

Characteristic of the readiness for martyrdom in this movement of the spirit (and of Methodius himself, who was to die a martyr's death in the year 311) is the cry of these fire-bearing virgins:

Fleeing the cunning serpent's
Thousandfold flatteries,
I endure the firebrand's flame
And the dread onslaught of wild beasts,
To await thy coming from heaven.

The purifying effect of fire

To expect Christ is to be ready for the fire in the strength of the flaming Spirit. Jesus baptizes with the Holy Spirit and with fire. Whoever arms himself for the expectation of God's kingdom prepares himself in his spirit for the fire-baptism of martyrdom. With the spiritual fire of judgment and light of love, Jesus brings to earth the fire of the burnt offering, a fire of purification through utmost suffering. As the bitter Christ, he brings the salting fire of extreme need. Making ready for the burnt offering, his fire seasons. Defying persecution and death by fire, the blazing torch of his mission calls for the ultimate sacrifice.

"Everyone, everyone, must be salted with fire." "You must not be surprised at the burning fire. It burns for your purification." "The time has come for judgment to begin with the household of God." Faith, like gold, must pass the final test by fire. God tests hearts through need and suffering as fire tests silver. The coming day will disclose what each one has been building. God's day is revealed in a fire that melts everything. All that the nations have labored over comes into the burning fire. God will pick out the

Matt. 3:11

Matt. 20:22–23

Mark 9:49

1 Pet. 4:12

1 Pet. 4:17

1 Pet. 1:7

Prov. 17:3

1 Cor. 3:12–13

gold and the silver in the smelting flame. His burning   Prov. 17:3
is like a goldsmith's fire.

The purifying effect of fire and its power to ward
off all animals and nocturnal spirits have been
obvious to man from time immemorial. The fire-
beacons at springtime and Easter, like the fires at the
midsummer and midwinter solstices, were meant
to cleanse the land and the springs of water and set
them free from all powers of evil. The fire-baptism
of the Spirit of Jesus Christ, the cleansing fire that
banishes everything unclean and malevolent, brings
purification through need and suffering and, above
all, through the fire of judgment in church discipline.[19]

In the light of the believing church everything
destructive and selfish is continually sorted out by
the fire and rejected. Everything that cannot stand
before the purity of the holy flame is thrown out
and swept away. The mystery of the church is Christ   Eph. 4:22–33
shining in her. The pure fire of the Holy Spirit is
proof of Christ's presence. His clear light tolerates no
defilement. The mystery of the church is the purified
expectation of God's coming glory and majesty. The
light world of the coming kingdom tolerates no darkening of the waiting church. The pure light of God
allows no darkness to approach his lampstands.

The light of Christ within you
The believers in Israel of the Old Testament testified:
"The Lord is my light." They called to God, "May thy   Ps. 27:1
countenance shine upon me!" They knew about living   Num. 6:25
in the sight of God's shining eyes and let themselves

---

19 For Arnold's understanding of church discipline, see the chapter "Admo-
nition and Forgiveness" in *God's Revolution* (Plough, 2021), 108–114.

be guided by his light and his truth. They came to the recognition: "In thy light do we see light." The light knows nothing but light and refuses to let its purity be impaired. The prophet proclaims: what the light shines upon shall become light. "Arise! Shine! For thy light has come; the radiant glory of Jehovah has risen upon thee." Where there is light, everything shines. Light wishes to be light and remain light without any darkening.

Yet the believers of the old covenant lacked the secret that was entrusted to Paul, the apostle of the gentiles: that radiance alive in the church, the radiance of glory to come, which in its inner aspect is in fact the light of the "Christ within you"! The innermost becomes one with the outermost and with the ultimate. The light burning on the lampstand of the church proclaims the death of Christ, his second coming, and the future world. It proclaims the burnt offering of the present time as well as the universal conflagration of the last day.

The prayer of the apostle is that Christ dwell in our hearts through faith. Jesus Christ, the resplendent reflection of God's radiant majesty, gives light for God's kingdom. He is the true light, which enlightens all people and shines into their darkness. He brings each one to the crucial decision whether he or she loves darkness more than light or wants to turn from darkness to light. When this happens, a sudden and wonderful change takes place in those about to be born anew. It shows the stark contrast: formerly, in and of themselves, they had been "darkness"; now, in Christ, they become "light." They come to the light of the world. They see the light. They are saved from the ruling powers of darkness so that

Ps. 36:9

Eph. 5:13

Isa. 60:1

Col. 1:27

Eph. 3:17

Rev. 1:12–13

John 1:5–9

John 3:19

Acts 26:18

Eph. 5:8

from then on the fire of unity, as the light of peace,
rules in them. "Just as fire sets iron aglow, just as the
sun at work on a plant makes it bright and glossy, so
Christ rules the surrendered will and gives man new
birth as a heavenly creature."[20]

"Wherever a man surrenders himself completely,
a spark of divine energy falls like burning tinder into
the center of his life-structure. This spark gives its
strength to set his whole life aflame with the fire that
Adam had let dwindle to dark and lifeless coals. The
light of divine energy is kindled in this fire. Thus the
created being is no longer his own property but the
instrument of God's Spirit."[21] Out of this rulership
of inner light, a life of light takes shape that includes
everything, transforming all previous confusion into
clarity. It excludes the works of darkness. It leads to
the works of burning light: self-consuming deeds   Rom. 13:12
of love sending out rays far and wide. Even Eckhart
recognized the dynamic effect of light when he said:
"In this birth, God pours himself into man's soul with
so much light that in man's essence and nature there
is an abundance of light. As a result, it bursts out
and overflows into all his energies and even into his
outward appearance."[22] Light is clarity and effective
action. As the mystery of the "Christ within you" at
work in the enlightened heart, the inner light brings
clarity about Christ and his work, about our inner
being, about evil the world over, and about how to
conduct life in both attitude and deed in accordance
with the source of light.

---

20 Jakob Böhme in Wiesenhütter, *Morgenröte*, 69.

21 Jakob Böhme in Wiesenhütter, *Morgenröte*, 83.

22 Meister Johannes Eckhart, c. 1260–c. 1327, *Meister Eckharts mystische
Schriften*, edited by Gustav Landauer (Axel Junckers Buchhandlung,
1903), 24.

Enlightenment comes from light's source

Light is clarity; it never wishes to bring gloomy uncertainty with it. A witness to light must be clear and definite. Mechthild of Magdeburg often spoke of the "streaming light of the divinity,"[23] yet even her words suffer from a certain cloudiness. She speaks more of the broadened stream than of the generously flowing source. The light of the moon does not prevent us from recognizing very clearly all its hills and mountains and the whole of the surface turned toward us. The moon withdraws from our view only as far as it sinks into darkness. When we study the sun, we can look into its depths in spite of all its radiant brightness. To the eye searching in these depths, the sun reveals its heart whenever it opens up before us in whirling solar storms. Every light radiates from a source, the giver of its energy. True enlightenment must reach the final goal of grasping the light bearer himself. It is the nature of light to reveal itself directly and without intermediary. The more refractions and reflections the light has gone through, the more noticeably is it changed and weakened when we receive it. We must dare to look the shining sphere straight in the face. We must receive it into ourselves as it is.

The mystic's concept of submerging into darkness and unconsciousness is poles apart from the apostolic enlightenment given to Paul; through the Spirit, Paul is able to recognize who God is and what his heart is. The inner light of the Spirit penetrates to the very depths of the Godhead. It reveals to our spirit what no eye has seen and no ear has heard – what has never

---

23 Mechthild of Magdeburg, 1212–1299, *Das fliessende Licht der Gottheit.*

entered the heart of man. Only light sees light. "We   1 Cor. 2:9
cannot grasp even the smallest spark of light unless
the burning Spirit of God himself enters our soul
like a fire."[24] "There would be nothing to catch the
sun's brightness if in the depths there were not the
same nature as the sun." Only the pure light of divine
power gives us sight. "There has to be something
present to catch the light of the sun. It is the star in
your eyes." Christ, as the morning star in your heart,   2 Pet. 1:19
sees within you the sun of the future. We ourselves
do not have this power of vision. The inner light can
see deep into eternity only because it is more than
reason, more than human ability, more even than the
deepest depths of the human conscience. It is in very
truth the Spirit of the Son of Man in the believer, the
Spirit far superior to our reasoning, who recognizes
God's Spirit. He alone sees. He is the light in the eye,
the seeing pupil of the eye, who proclaimed himself
as the light that illuminates. The light kindles life   John 8:12
in the one who sees. To the inner eye, Jesus Christ
shines as the ultimate reality of God's new creation.
As God's creative, illuminating clarity, as ultimate
decisiveness, which is his nature, he penetrates into
the perceptive heart. As the shining tree of life and
knowledge, he spreads his roots into the depths,
and his branches afar. The root is the spirit of joy
that leaps up when life is kindled. "When the soul is
kindled by the Holy Spirit, it triumphs in the body,
and a great fire of new life flares up in the soul."

The origin of this illuminating light is the pure
clarity of its source, of its bearer. Recognizing
it always depends on the inconceivable contrast

---

24 Quotations in this paragraph are from Jakob Böhme in Wiesenhütter,
   Morgenröte.

between this light and the darkness of human life. The meaning of darkness can be detected only in the light. Darkness is shown up only when it is dispelled by light, and without a dispelling of darkness there is no knowledge of the source of light. When light is accepted, it brings liberation and redemption. Forgiveness is the removal of the darkening powers of night. When the land is flooded with radiant brightness, the landscape of human life is purified from the works and creatures of darkness. Then land and life enter into the community of light. Darkness is banned. Creation, redeemed, shines resplendent in the worship of God's holy mountain, which pours forth light because the heart of God's light dwells there. Through the light of this holy mountain, everything that used to live in darkness will be led back into the bright community of God's heart.

Luke 11:35–36

We experience the Lord of Light through the light that streams out from him. Whoever sees him in the light, sees him as he is. In the coming world of light, all works and all life will be transformed by the inner vision into his nature, which is light. "Then the sun and the stars will pass away; for the heart will shine as the light of God and fill everything. When God's heart triumphs, everything will rejoice."[25] Until this transformation takes place, the believing church of today must be led onward step by step from her present imperfect recognition to the ultimate vision, she must be led more and more deeply into the mystery of God's heart. She must learn in Jesus Christ how to distinguish between the footsteps of God – which show his judgment making the history of nations – and the inmost heart of God.

25 Jakob Böhme in Wiesenhütter, *Morgenröte*, 272.

Christ's kingdom is not of this world

The brothers called Hutterians (after Jakob Hutter) have known from their very beginning to the present day how to distinguish between the ultimate depths of light in God's heart and the mighty consequences of his flaming wrath. Along with their spokesman Peter Riedemann, they have given a particularly clear testimony, especially in their *Great Article Book* and *Confession of Faith*.[26] They maintain that whereas the rod of his wrath must punish profligate nations still today, in Christ God's wrath has long since come to an end. In Christ has begun the quite other kingdom of blessings, the quite other rule of love and kindness. "Wherever blessing comes, or has already come, wrath comes to an end."[27]

Whoever is unaware of this difference will not be able to come to an understanding of God's light. In Christ alone is the whole blessing of God's heart revealed – only Christ himself is the blessing of perfect love. Therefore what is still ordained under the curse of wrath, under the mercilessness of fierce judgment, has no place whatsoever in Christ. And vice versa: the child of blessing and love can never be the servant of wrath and vengeance. What the Father has ordained in Christ will remain in Christ and will never be changed. It is love, peace, unity, and community. What God has appointed outside his Christ, however, is death, wrath, mercilessness, curse, and vengeance – all this cannot continue, as the prophet Hosea declared so sternly about the power

Hos. 14:4–9

1 John 2:9–11

---

26 *Great Article Book* attributed to Peter Walpot (1521–1578) and *Peter Riedemann's Hutterite Confession of Faith* (1542) translated and edited by John J. Friesen (Plough, 2019).

27 *Peter Riedemann's Hutterite Confession of Faith*, 221.

of governmental authority: "I have given you a king in my anger, and I have taken him away again in my wrath."

Hos. 13:11

Christ is the opposite of all world rulers. His kingdom is not of this world. Therefore he said: "The princes and powers of this world lord it over the people, but you should not." A Christian, therefore, is not a ruler, and a ruler is not a Christian. A ruler must exercise judgment with the sword. In the church of Christ there is an end of war and violence, lawsuits and legal action. Christ does not repay evil with evil. His followers show his nature in all their doings. They act as he did: they do not resist evil, and they give their backs to the smiters and their cheeks to those who pluck off the hair. Their task is to reveal the kingdom of love. Legal authorities are appointed to shed blood in judgment; the church of Christ, however, has the task of preserving life and soul. The law courts of the state must bring evil to account; the church of Jesus Christ must repay evil with good. The authorities that sit in judgment must hate and persecute the enemies of their order; the church of Christ must love them.

John 18:36
Matt. 20:25–26
Phil. 2:1–18
Matt. 5:39–48
Isa. 50:6
Rom. 12:17
Rom. 13:1–7

With governmental authority as an instrument, God's wrath punishes the wicked. Through the authorities, he compels nations that are estranged from him to protect themselves from the worst harm so that the whole land does not become guilty of bloodshed, so that the whole earth does not have to be destroyed. Christ gives his church a completely different task. She must confront the forcible execution of justice in the world state with the peace of unity and the joy of love, with brotherly justice. She

John 13:34–35

builds up and maintains her unity with no other
tools than those of love and the Spirit. In the faith of
the church, death and the law come to an end. The
freedom of the kingdom of God begins in the church.   Gal. 5

Those who are grafted into Christ demonstrate
the mind and the spirit of Christ as unchangeable
love. They do what is good and do not need to fear   John 15
the forcible execution of punishment over evil, nor do
they need to exercise it. Punishment, which belongs
to power and judgment, is quite alien to Christ and
his church, like all the evil that calls for this punishment. In Christ, the inmost heart of God's love frees
itself from the historically necessary wrath and world
judgment, in which God has to assert the holiness of
his will through the force of the law.

God's wrath and God's love

A hundred years after this had been recognized by
the Hutterian brothers and put into words by Peter
Riedemann, Jakob Böhme (who, like Riedemann, was
a Silesian cobbler) tried to grasp the depths of this
far-reaching recognition. He saw it as the difference
between God's fire of wrath and his heart of light:
God is love and wrath, light and fire, yet he calls
himself God according to the light of his love alone,
not according to his wrath. Whatever does not belong
to his love belongs to his wrath. Yet God is not called
God according to his whole nature but according to
the light; he dwells in himself with light alone.

The outward person lives among the thorns of
God's wrath. The love of God, as light, dwells in itself.
The darkness does not comprehend it or know any-
thing about it. The eternal rulership of God according   Ps. 82:5
to love and wrath, light and fire, is to be revealed in

Deut. 32:22

Jer. 17:4

Isa. 30:27–28

the life of man, which stands in this conflict. In the darkness, God is a God of wrath and a devouring fire: darkness calls for fire. If it were possible for darkness to be lit from the light directly, the light would have no root; if it were not possible to produce fire, there would be no light either. For this reason, the kingdom of fury has to be; wrath is the cause of the fire world as judgment over darkness. It lives in darkness. It is not called God but the wrath of God.

Luke 10:18

Matt. 4:1–11

The devil kindled the wrath of God. He wanted to have his own will; he wanted to be his own god in order to rule as he wished in and over everyone with the mighty power of fire. The nature of his fire is choleric; it produces daring boldness, furious wrath, and mounting pride; it always wants to rule, which is typical of power. Severity, harshness, fear, torment, and unpeace are part of it. This fire-will brings fear. Without this fear, fire would not exist. It was in God's wrath that the devil forfeited love. In the fire-will, the devil and God meet face to face. The powers of wrath, of judgment, and of the sword are pagan. They remain far from the heart of God. They can never be Christian. And yet they have been appointed by God, for God's holy majesty would not exist if his wrath did not exist, which salts and seasons the darkness so that it is transformed into fire.

2 Chron. 25:13

As war and violence, this wrath burning between God and the devil consumes all that is godless. Every soldier is a rod of God's wrath. God's judgment in its fury punishes people through him. The soldier belongs to the order of fury through which God's wrath sets up and tears down countries and kingdoms. Wood that is becoming dry calls for fire.

God's wrath has always existed, just as fire lies hidden Jer. 10:10
in wood. As soon as the wood dried out – as soon as
self-will turned away from God's heart – the burning
had to begin.

Yet God wanted a supreme light of love to be born
out of the consuming blaze of murderous fire. That
other majesty of God – the utter sublimity of his
heart – was to be revealed in this light. The somber
fire of wrath is not God but a hellish fire. Yet if there Rev. 13:7
were no fire, no light would be given. God's fire of
wrath becomes the root of his compassionate love, Ps. 90
that is, of the light in his heart. In the critical times
of his judgment, his love shall become manifest. In
the fullness of God's time, the last judgment will
become the wedding feast of his kingdom of love. The
fire is overpowered by the light. Out of the burning
torment, a sublime kingdom of joy shall arise. As 2 Cor. 5
soon as a burning fire blazes up, light shines out.
The light takes on all the vital characteristics of
fire: it awakens life, it draws people together so that
they find each other, and it leads to the God-given
community of the circle, the encampment, and the
consecrated house.

It has simply become a question of decision
between love in light and blazing wrath in darkness.
In light, God is a merciful and loving God; only in the
strength of light is he called God. The light world, 1 John 1:5–7
which is God himself, has no craving for destruction.
There is no spark in God's heart that could desire Ezek. 18:23
evil, even as punishment! In God a great joy of love 1 Tim. 2:3–4
surges out of the wellspring of his heart. Thus the
fight for man arises. God's heart wants him because
he is meant to be God's image and likeness; the

kingdom of wrath wants him too, because he now belongs to the very nature of darkness. The soul of man once left the paradise of love for the fiery life of wrath. So this soul of man died to God's light, perishing in selfhood, in possessions. It died to God and lived in utter fear of his stern wrath. Yet the ray of light came once more to the soul and said:

Gen. 3

Acquire the love of God in your heart so that out of the heart of God you will be born again in the center of your life. The light of his heart shall send light into your life! You shall become one with him! You had willfully broken away from my love and fallen into the fiery clutches of wrath. Now I will shed my rays of love with bright light into your fear-ridden life of fire. As love, I will transform the fire of your fear into the open flame of my joy. As the essence of light, I will impart my rays of love into your life and work, renewing them with light.[28]

1 Cor. 15:45–49
Phil. 3:20–21

The kingdom of light and love

So from the heart of God the life of light, full of joy, shines with power into all powers and sets them on fire for the work of love. The will is gathered to give birth to light. Lit by God's light, the inner vision breaks swiftly through, keen as a flash of lightning; it soars up from the heart and catches fire in the will to love; it is no longer furious lightning but a power of great joy. Christ is this joy. What has arisen in the enlightened heart is the joyous light of the Son of God as the fire of love. From now on, the life that gives outward expression to such a heart should reveal the inmost spirit of the light world in all it

---

28 Jakob Böhme in Wiesenhütter, *Morgenröte*, 282, 285–286, paraphrased.

does; the essence of this light is the kingdom of God.   Eph. 5:8–10
From the most inward and tender love of Christ
arises the kingdom of joy.

True faith in the kingdom of God is the power,
spirit, and life of a shining light, welling up from the
heart of God. It is the supreme power of God, real and
living, the flaming love that shines out of his heart.
His work is accomplished by this love. The essential
part of faith, burning in the believing Christian as
strength that also loves, is Christ himself, who is the
life and light of the renewed person. The love of the
church is faith in the heart of God, who pours his sea
of light into all lands.

Christ is the joyful urge to love, coming from a
flood of light that gains dominion over wrath's urge
for fire. After the soul forfeited light, God spoke the
name "Jesus." In him, God's wrath is extinguished.
Christ is the heart of God, triumphing over all the
consequences of God's wrath and hastening to all
lands met by it. Christ sends his light into all the
world; it rises over all nations and shines on them
without partiality. Even to the most godless, gripped   Isa. 9:1–2
in consuming fire by the violent wrath of God, the
gates of birth into light stand open.

The light of love displaces the fire of wrath

Through the death of Christ, Christians die to wrath
and its fierce decrees: they die with Christ to all the
elements of wrath. In Christ's spirit, in the love of
God's heart, those who live in that other justice of
loving forbearance have been reborn. Where once   Rom. 6
wrath burned in darkness, love is burning now, radiating from the shining heart of God. The fire of wrath

and the light of love are as alien as day and night. Neither understands the other; neither sees the other.

Yet from the very beginning, all human beings

Rom. 7:14–21 have both within them. It is just as if the right hand wants to enter into the majesty of light, and the left hand wants to stay in its original state – fire. Whichever of these two attributes is being awakened burns in people: the soul can burn with the light of love or

Matt. 6:24 with the fire of wrath. If it surrenders to wrath, wrath spreads like a cancer and subjects everything to the laws it makes in avenging fury. But if it surrenders to the heart in God, it learns that the Holy Spirit of Jesus Christ dwelling there knows no wrath, wages no war, and administers no violent punishment – he only

1 Cor. 13 loves and gives.

The wisdom of God's heart has no desire for death or war. The children of God's heart may not kill or

Matt. 5:38–48 go to war. They need no murderous weapons. No one who is a Christian can go to war. Whoever does, does it as a heathen within the order of wrath, never as a Christian within the order of love.[29] Countries and cities are laid waste in war only where the relentless cycle of guilt and vengeance, of offense and retaliation, strangles and murders and kills. In Christ, the vicious cycle of cause and effect is abolished.

Mars grows pale and vanishes as soon as the sun rises. Lightning storms retreat before a sunlit sky. The heart of God disperses the clouds of his wrath: even in the midst of judgment, his heart triumphs over his wrath. Led by this heart, the church of Jesus Christ passes through history's fires of wrath without being in contact with them. She is dead to the world

---

29 Jakob Böhme in Wiesenhütter, *Morgenröte*, 252.

of wrath's elements; they can do nothing to harm her, and she stands quite apart from them. Because they are all rooted in darkness, the church of light keeps her back turned on all their characteristics.

The church has died to greed for property (the ultimate root of all evil) and the pride and respect that go with it. She has left behind her all fear and insincerity, unfaithfulness and covetousness, those ugly, monstrous offspring of the fires of hell. She abominates the heart and will of mammon, who rules the world, the great antigod who uses war and strife to build up societies and classes, kingdoms and countries, in order to shatter them again. The church discerns the spirits. She knows what she is waiting for, what she loves, and what she believes in. She knows what she has left behind and can never take up again.

1 Tim. 6:10

1 John 4:1

Christ dwells in his church

The church stands in the dawn of the coming day. Therefore she cannot take part in the works of nocturnal darkness that rule the world, nor can she take part in the blazing wrath of fiery judgment on the world of today. It is in Christ that she lives, and she dwells in God's heart. She does the work of love; she believes in and waits for the reign of light. Her members are weak, but the spirit that dwells in her is the shining fire of God's heart. True, the plant cannot say "I am the sun" because the sun is at work in it. And quite certainly, the believing members of the church cannot say "I am Christ" because Christ dwells in them and is at work in them. But the believing church shall be transformed into the image of

2 Cor. 3:18

his radiant beauty insofar as she looks with unveiled face upon his being. The vision given to faith, like the transformation to come, is an enlightenment that springs from the heart of God. Christ, the future Lord of the eternal light world, reveals himself in his wonderful light as the spirit of his church.

Christ dwells at one and the same time in the shining throne of God's heart and in the Spirit-filled body of his church. About the year 1000, Simeon,[30] addressing a hymn to God out of this experience, has an important word to say about the church of light, this new body of the Spirit, and about the enlightenment of her members:

> Your whole body, unspotted, divine, uncompounded, and yet compounded in an inexpressible way, flashes with the fire of your divinity; that is what you have given me, my God. He is in my heart yet dwells in heaven; both here and there I see him in the same shining light. For me he is present and shines in my poor heart, clothes me in immortal glory, and shines through all my members. I have become a partaker of the light, a partaker of the glory, and my countenance shines like that of him who is my desire; I have the creator of all things with me! Honor and glory be to him now and in eternity.

2 Cor. 4:6

God himself, who let light shine out of darkness in his Son, has "caused a bright light to shine in our hearts to give the light of the knowledge of God's glory as we see it in the face of Jesus Christ." In the quickening spirit of his church, we can see his bright radiance face to face. The image of his love is bound to grow

---

30 Simeon of Trier, d. 1035, monk and hermit.

dim where dogmas, however good, are merely learned by heart; where the Bible is read only literally; and where obedience remains outward obedience only. As the inner eye of the community of believers becomes brighter and livelier, it becomes more and more open to enlightenment in the uniting Spirit of Jesus Christ and increasingly able to grasp the exuberant greatness of his radiant power. For the most faithful in Ephesus Paul prays for the enlightened eyes of understanding. Only those who have Jesus himself in their hearts as an illuminating light can gain strength and clarity from God, who reveals the infinite life and power of light in the church of Jesus Christ. Eph. 1:15–21

Through inner enlightenment, the Lord of Light reveals himself to us. This is inextricably bound up with growing clarity about the true way, which leads in the full light of truth to God's final objective. "Awake, O sleeper, and arise from the dead, and Christ shall give you light." This rousing call of the Spirit goes with an urgent challenge to lead the life given only to children of light. It is a matter of the new life and growth of the church, which must itself be described as a light, for it lives in unity with Christ: "You are the light of the world," for the Christ of the final kingdom is your Lord. He is the light of the whole world here and now in his church. Eph. 5:14

Matt. 5:14

John 8:12

Light tolerates no darkness

This light tolerates no community with the barren works of darkness. Both in the innermost recesses of the heart and in the outer aspects of life, it exposes everything that is secret or shameful or that has a bad effect. "Everything exposed by the light becomes visible" – the action of light discloses and transforms everything – "and everything that is illuminated becomes a light." Light is clarity. Therefore what believers of old experienced is renewed in the light of Jesus Christ: "Thou hast set our iniquities before thee, our secret sins in the light of thy countenance!" Light unlocks the doors of night. It encourages honest openmindedness, the only state in which a person can become convicted of sin. God brings about an openheartedness that leads to absolute decisiveness: in order to be renewed in the light of Jesus Christ for the life of his church, we give room to light, do away with all that is dark as something to be hated, and recognize and leave behind the depressing feelings of guilt that shackled us.

Eph. 5:11–13
Ps. 90:8

Light does not work like dynamite, yet it is stronger. The weapons of light fight without any murderous force against the works of darkness. Love does no evil to its neighbor. And nevertheless, at the eleventh hour before the coming day, it puts an end to the waxing powers of night and their violent works. Anyone who wants to put a dark cover over his hostile actions can pile up as many mountains of dark, hateful thoughts and deeds as he likes: we know that there are rays that in all quietness penetrate even the thickest walls of the strongest fortresses. When the working of the Spirit's light is perfect, it has latent in it a power to remove and overcome that is stronger than all the forces of destruction.

Rom. 13:10–12

One of the most remarkable discoveries is that of the momentum of light. Every perpendicular ray of light exercises a pressure that is quiet, gentle, and firm, in keeping with the nature of light. This is how astronomers explain why the tail of a comet turns away from the sun. When the dark and distant comet nears the sun, clouds begin to form out of its head, through the action of solar heat. The sun's radiation pressure blows these vapors away from the head, producing the long tail. The light of the sun repels the expanding vapor. It destroys nothing. But when another body approaches, the light quietly and almost imperceptibly drives anything it cannot tolerate in its vicinity out of the center of that body.

Unless we turn to the Sun of the universe, we remain in the dark. "If the light that is in you is darkness, how great is the darkness then?" Unless Matt. 6:23 we hasten with open eyes toward the divine light, we remain blind. Just as a man who is blind from birth can never find a substitute for his eyesight through his intellect, so we can never be led to inner light through our powers of reasoning. Only when the power of the sun opens our inner eye, can we see the light that shines down upon us from the distant presence of God.

Faith is a light from God

Faith is a light from God that surpasses all human understanding. The light of faith is God himself drawing near and intervening. Anyone who stands in the sun has no lack of light. Everything becomes clear and bright as soon as the inner eye is enlightened and "sound," focused on the one ruler of the central fire. It Matt. 6:22 is given to the eye of faith to see and understand the perfect light. "If the eye were not in its nature like the sun, it could never see the sun."[31] "Therefore see to

31 Johann Wolfgang von Goethe, 1749–1832, *Zahme Xenien 3.*

it that the light that is in you is not darkness! When your body has no single particle of darkness left in it, it will be completely light, as if you were illuminated by a bright flash of lightning!"

Luke 11:35–36

God's enlightenment draws near with elemental force. Unforgettable are those moments in which a flash of lightning lays bare the deep-black mantle of night, exposing every hiding place and bringing to light all the vermin of darkness – those predators of the night that would flee from every ray of light. "He who does evil hates the light. He does not want to come to the light lest his works be punished." Yet greater than lightning at night is the sight of the rising sun, especially where the contrast between night and day is not veiled by our northern twilight. Life awakens with the light. Birds of daylight sing, flowers of the light open, and the whole land is radiant with the glory of the morning. This is what happens when God's morning star heralds the sunrise of life. Whoever longs for light is open to it. Whoever loves light hastens toward it. "Whoever lives by the truth comes to the light so that his works may be clearly seen, for they have been done in God."

John 3:20

John 3:21

Walk in the light

The light is the exposer, the liberator, the leader. The inner light begins to lead the whole of life where a life in God begins, where the inner and outer life go to meet Christ's shining countenance, where his power dispels darkness. The believing church finds the way that leads to the kingdom of light. It lies clearly in front of her. "If a man walks in the daytime, he does not stumble, for he sees the light that lights the world. If a man walks at night, however, he stumbles because

he has no light." The way has to be well lit if we are   John 11:9–10
to find it. The light wishes to bring our entire way of
life into one single, very clearly defined direction. It
wishes to lead our whole life on the one way that is
the only way into the kingdom of God.

Words of eternal truth testify to this influence
on the direction of our life and work: we must work
while it is day. When the dark night comes, no one   John 9:4
can work. Jesus says, therefore:

> As long as I am in the world, I am the light of the   John 9:5
> world.
>   I am the light of the world. Whoever follows me
> will never walk in darkness but will have the light of   John 8:12
> life.
>   Walk while you have the light, so that the
> darkness may not overtake you. If you walk in the
> darkness, you do not know where you are going.
> While you have the light, believe in the light, so that   John 12:35–36
> you may become children of light.

Even the people of the old covenant knew that "the
path of the righteous is like the glorious light of
morning that grows brighter and brighter until it is
broad daylight! The way of the lawless is like darkness; they do not know what makes them stumble and
fall." Being divinely led by this guiding light means   Prov. 4:18–19
being protected from the deceptive bypaths and will-
o'-the-wisps of night. From his wellspring of light,
God has given clear vision to steer the right course.
With this vision the way cannot be missed. For those
nights when the sky is overcast, a bright lantern is
put into the traveler's hand: the Word of God, which
lights the dark way ahead until the day dawns and the   2 Pet. 1:19
morning star rises!

Through the Word, Jesus Christ reveals himself as the guiding light to the people of the new covenant. He is the fulfillment of the words of old: "The commandments of the Lord shine clear and give light to the eyes." "Thy word is a lamp to my feet and a light on my path." Guidance through the inner light of the Spirit of Jesus Christ is accomplished through the lamp of the Word. Nevertheless, his truth bears a new criterion, decisive for this present age, one that proves the purity and unity of the guiding light: the unanimity of the church of Christ throughout all ages. In the church, God lets his thoughts of light be known without deflection. The church of Jesus Christ is the city of light: its foundation is community through the mystery shining in her.

Ps. 19:8

Ps. 119:105

John 17:21–23

In Reformation times, the church that had once been the early Christian church set up the lamp of her unifying light again in the midst of severe persecution. After Jakob Hutter's death, decisive words of truth were given to his fellow worker Peter Riedemann:

> The church of Christ is a foundation and a basis of truth. It is a lamp, a star of light, and a lantern of righteousness, in which the light of grace is held up to the whole world, so that its darkness, unbelief, and blindness may be illuminated, and people may learn to see and know the way of life. So we see that the church of Christ is, in the first place, like a lantern completely filled with light, the light of Christ, which is then shed abroad to others.
>
> As the lantern of Christ has been made bright and clear by the light of the knowledge of God, so

its radiance shines out into the distance to give light
to those who still walk in darkness. Christ himself
commanded this when he said, "Let your light shine
before others, that they may see your good works,
and praise God, the Father in heaven." Now this can
take place only through the strength of the Spirit of
Christ working within us.

Just as a light, in accordance with its own nature,
sends out a beam to give light to people, so also the
divine light, wherever it has been lit in a person,
sends forth its divine ray according to its nature.
The nature of this light, however, is genuine divine
righteousness, holiness, and truth. It sheds its light
abroad more brightly and clearly than the sun to
enlighten all people.[32]

This was given to the apostle of Jesus Christ, as he
himself testified: to bring light to all people about the
mystery of the church, which is inseparably bound
up with the mystery of the coming Christ. The inner
light of Jesus Christ reveals the oneness between his
nature and the unity of the church with its future
destiny. Enlightenment through the Holy Spirit has
the unmistakable characteristic of leading to complete
unanimity, to undisturbed harmony and agreement
between all the members of the church of light.

The light of God's heart reveals the mystery of
the church: the church is the radiant body of Jesus
Christ. This body cannot be dark – its eye is clear and
bright. Focused on the center of its field of vision,
its eye receives the light. Christ himself in all his
radiance, and nothing else, dwells in this body. He is
the faith of the church. His future is what she awaits.

Matt. 5:16

Matt. 10:27
Eph. 3:8–12

Col. 1:12–18

---

32 *Peter Riedemann's Hutterite Confession of Faith*, 78.

She is filled here and now with the future rays of his majesty. The hope of her life is to extol his glory.

Professing Christendom and its mission can experience rebirth only through the living church of love and light. The people of light are gathered by the torch of the one leader in order that he may establish his sun-kingdom with them. Only the lamps of the church can show the light of the future to earth's darkness. The Spirit of Jesus Christ, as the light that from now on determines everything, rests on these seven lamps. From these lamps goes out the transforming power of God's approaching future:

Rev. 1:12–20
Rev. 2:1

> Thou radiant morning sun,
> Thou dost consume the flames!
> Thou art the joy of burning fire,
> Victorious in thy mighty course![33]

---

33 From Arnold's poem "Das Dunkle ist vergangen," *Poems and Rhymed Prayers* (Plough, 2003), 260–263.

The Holy Spirit

Which spirit will you serve?

The gift of inwardness is a two-edged sword. Litera-
ture shows that there are people who want to fathom
not only God and his truth, but just as much Satan
and his abyss. Which do you want – God or the devil?
A decision must be made. God is good, and he is
spirit. The realm of the evil spirit is the demonic. Do
you want to submerge yourself into both at the same
time? You can recognize a spiritual being only by
becoming one with it: there is no other way of com-
prehending a spirit than by uniting with the essence John 17:20–21
of its innermost nature. Here you are, a living person: 1 Cor. 6:17
Which spirit do you want to unite with? After long
years of indecision on this question, Augustine made
up his mind: "God and my soul are what I want to
understand. Nothing else? No, nothing else!"[1]

The human soul is dominated by flesh and blood.
With one hand it grasps at life; with the other it
grasps at death. As Friedrich Nietzsche said, "Woe to

---

1 Augustine of Hippo, 354–430, bishop and theologian, *Soliloquies*, Book I.

the man who has no ground under his feet! Woe to the man who has no support!"[2] "This is the danger I slip into: my vision soars up to the heights while my hand wants to keep hold of the depths and find

Rom. 7:18 support there."[3] We have started out on a dangerous journey because the life-giving Spirit of the heights and the life-hating spirits of the abyss are fighting a hard battle over us. On this journey, human nature in its own strength is incapable of lifting itself above the level of flesh and blood. The soul can turn its gaze inward as much as it likes or the heart look to some great national ideal, but without the Spirit of God they stay on the all-too-human lowlands of mortal blood.

Because our spirit is so closely bound up with our psychophysical makeup, it comes under the same judgment as our body: "What is born of the flesh

John 3:6 is flesh." Flesh is bound to decay. The horrors of our time have shown what harvest is reaped when the seed of life is cast upon the soil of unchanged

Rom. 8:13 human nature. Only the harvest blown upon by the

Gal. 6:8 wind of the life-giving Spirit will be good. Without the Holy Spirit, human nature remains dull and feeble. Without the wind of the Spirit, the tilled field of human nature remains barren. Cut off from the fountainhead and drying up in its independence, the life of human nature is doomed to destruction. Our nature is debased – we ought to know how degenerate and desecrated it is.

Mortal nature longs for a superior power to free enslaved humankind from all powers hostile to life. Only the Spirit of perfect life has this power

---

2 Friedrich Nietzsche, 1844–1900, "Der Freigeist" (1884).

3 Nietzsche, *Also sprach Zarathustra*.

to overcome death. Without this divine Spirit who overcame all deadening and evil spirits, we are lost. God and his Spirit alone are life. The Spirit of the Son redeems us from bondage and fear of death; only he can give full and abiding life. Those who are unable to discriminate between the Spirit and the voice of the blood condemn themselves to remain sensual beings; as enslaved beings, they remain in bondage to their corrupting nature and its murderous powers.

John 6:63
Rom. 8:1–2

People who lay decisive value on the sensual impulses of their blood are described by Paul as carnal, even if they are able to probe the depths of inwardness or rise to the loftiest ideals of their nation or of humanity. The soul by itself, like the blood, is always limited to the mortal life of individuals and their nation. Throughout the whole of humankind, it is conditioned by the body and subject to demons. And yet the soul knows that deep down it has a disposition created for higher and purer spheres. The conscience continually bears witness:

Rom. 8:5–9

Col. 2:18

> A man! Yes, only he is worthy of the name
> Who lifts his spirit high above the human plane.[4]

The Holy Spirit is stronger than other spirits

Without Jesus Christ, we can never be more than a living soul. This enfeebled life leads itself toward death. Nations that let themselves be led by nothing but their racial community fall under the law of hate, which paves the way for death and for belonging to the kingdom of death. From humankind in general – as such – no help is to be expected. Only the one Son of Man is a life-giving spirit. His life is

1 Cor. 15:45–47

---

4 Angelus Silesius, *Cherubinischer Wandersmann.*

everlasting and overcomes all death. His strength is
the boundless power of unchangeable love; it releases
an inextinguishable vitality such as the immortal
Spirit alone can give. It leads mortal man to eternal
life. The Spirit of Jesus Christ is stronger than all
other spirits; he alone unites the believing heart with
the living center of all creative life.

In this center, the living Spirit creates the sublime
unity of all freed spirits, a unity that can be achieved
neither by nations nor by humankind. The Holy
Spirit is this unity in Christ – he brings about a
united life in God. He alone guarantees one people
and one kingdom – that is, God's people and God's
kingdom – as an eternal inheritance. Only the Spirit
of the great liberator can give that eternal reality to
the human spirit in which the children of all peoples
are children of the one God. God's people comes
into being in the Holy Spirit. Only in him does true
humanity come into existence. In the power of this
life-giving Spirit, God's firstborn was shown to be
his Son. As the risen Christ, he grants his people the
Spirit of his sonship. In him alone is the power of a
renewed and unified life. The king of the kingdom
is himself the life of God's people, the life in the
kingdom of God. Only he whose life was without any
inconsistency or hint of darkness brings the harmony
of the kingdom of God, without which all people and
all nations remain in the power of death and destruction, the power of the devil.

Christ alone is God's crowned one, so completely
inundated and penetrated by the Spirit that no spark
of his life was separated from the living flame of love.
This fiery life of the Spirit of Jesus Christ is the love

Eph. 4:3–6

1 Cor. 12:13

Rom. 1:4

Gal. 4:6

in the coming kingdom; his final kingdom is love as
justice. For this reason the life of Jesus, in holy fire,
belonged to the poor and wretched. Jesus is the only
one to whom the prophetic word of Isaiah applies
completely, and with it Jesus proclaimed his mes-
sianic mission: "The Spirit of the Lord is upon me. He
has anointed me king of the kingdom; he has sent me
to bring the poor a decisive message."

This anointing of Jesus is his coronation as ruler of
the kingdom, the imparting of the Spirit as the sovereign power of love, which alone brings true freedom.
His gospel is the joyful tidings of the coming
one, who leads to freedom all the oppressed and
enslaved – freedom for God's kingdom! In Jesus, the
king anointed by the Holy Spirit, the kingdom of God
has come to forsaken people in a world growing cold.
As perfect love it has come to drained and empty
hearts, in which the flame of love was trampled to the
ground by cold and sinister powers. The spirit of hate
had extinguished human love. In Jesus, the Spirit of
divine love overcomes the demonic spirit of servitude.
Jesus Christ is the one, the only one, who has driven
out the murderous spirit of this world and all his
subordinate spirits through the Spirit of perfect love.
Where the ruler of God's kingdom intervenes, their
rule comes to an end.

People held captive by their emotions and their
blood, however, perceive nothing of this decisive
action of the victorious Spirit. Only the Holy Spirit
himself recognizes the Holy Spirit. Without the
Spirit of God, no one can acknowledge the liberating
rule of Jesus Christ or see how he has already taken it
up for all time. Outside the Holy Spirit, the rule

Matt. 5:3

Isa. 61:1–2

Matt. 11:28

Matt. 12:27–28

1 Cor. 2:10–14

1 Cor. 12:3

of Jesus Christ and the power of love in it are not
given recognition. Only the Spirit reveals the divine
king and the freedom under his rulership; only in
the church of the Spirit is his kingdom at work on
earth today.

Only through the Holy Spirit, only in the spirit of
the church, can Christ be called upon as Lord and
king. In their uniting with the church, all those who
want truly to acknowledge Christ as their Lord must
have received the spirit of the church; they must be
immersed in the strength and reality of the Spirit
that creates the church. They must prove themselves
free children of the one pure Spirit in their common
action. Only in the unity of this one Spirit can they
call upon the holy Name in communal prayer.

The Holy Spirit establishes his work as God's work.
Only believers can grasp this. They should accept and
act upon it as God at work; they should bear it serenely
as God's doing. In the strength of another world
working in them, they acknowledge Christ as their
only Lord. In this Spirit, the voice from the eternal
throne answers them, "You call me Master and Lord;
and you say so rightly, for so I am." This recognition,
this testimony, can come to people (who in their
slavery are far removed from God) only when they
accept the Holy Spirit – a spirit not of men but of God.
The church covenant of this king and his kingdom
can be established, strengthened, or sealed in no other
way than through the Holy Spirit in a life lived in God.
From God, through Christ as the ruling Lord of God's
kingdom, he comes to a believing church.

Rom. 15:30

Acts 12:12

Phil. 2:13

John 13:13

2 Cor. 1:22

Christ sets enslaved people free

Only in this way will enslaved people become free
once and for all from any glorification of themselves
and from everything that dominates them from
without. There is freedom where the Spirit of the
king is. His covenant, which through faith in Jesus   John 8:32–36
Christ is eternally binding, separates the sons of
freedom from servile slaves. This difference is there
for all eternity. Those who are prompted by God's
Spirit have become God's free children; those who are   Rom. 8:14–17
not do not belong to God.

There are no slaves in God's church; all those who
live there are children of equal birth. The covenant
of sonship is established. All the unchildlikeness of
human greatness or degrading servitude is banned   Gal. 5:1
from this covenant. All its members are promised   Matt. 18:2–4
an amazing perception, granted only to trusting
children by virtue of the childlike spirit. It remains   Luke 10:21
closed to those who are great and wise in their own
estimation or enslaved by servile fear. God's Spirit
bears witness to and does what God has in mind for
everything free and childlike. When this covenant is
made, the superficiality and darkness of domineering
natures and servile subjection must disappear. In
the freedom of Jesus Christ their authority has been
broken forever.

The light opens up a life of childlike freedom,
strong and evident in its spirit. The slaves freed by
Christ now become his free property. Nothing that
is or might become theirs can belong to them or to
any other except him alone. In life and in death they
belong to their Master. As freed slaves who would   Rom. 14:8
have remained in ignoble servitude without his

intervention, they take their place with a freed will in
his household. They belong forever to the Spirit of his
house, with a right to his gifts as free children. They
honor their liberator as the only sovereign of the only
1 Cor. 7:23   kingdom they may serve.

The Holy Spirit is the pledge of a future
2 Cor. 5:5   inheritance, given by their royal liberator. With
the covenant of the Spirit in their hands, they have
a passport to the people's community of God's
Eph. 1:13–14   kingdom. The spirit of the church is a free pass and
certificate of citizenship for the kingdom of God.
When they show his seal, the gates of the final
kingdom are opened. All members of the church of
the Spirit seek him with their whole life. They love
and they live for the king of God's kingdom. They
strive for and believe in his freeing and uniting justice
and righteousness. In the Spirit of Jesus Christ, they
represent the perfect justice of the future. The Holy
Eph. 4:30   Spirit seals their faith in the king he has crowned.
This king has come in advance of his kingdom; in
him they have accepted its coming. As strength
arising from absolute freedom and unity, his justice
and righteousness are the ultimate reality of their
Rom. 14:17–18   lives. In the dynamic presence of the Spirit, they taste
the powers of a future world, of a different being
ruling their lives here on earth.

The Holy Spirit is God's seal
In the present age, the seal of the Holy Spirit is the
only valid assurance that the church of Christ has
become a partaker in the character and nature of
Heb. 3:14   God, a partaker in his future life. The Spirit of Christ
is certainty of God. The work of the Spirit, seen in

the power that comes from faith in the future, makes
the church firm and steadfast in all the storms of the
present day. In this Spirit she is certain that in his
own good time God will redeem the firm promise he
gave in Christ. Faith is as certain of this promise as if
it already has it; and in the reality of the Spirit, it does.   Heb. 11:1

Through the imparting of the Holy Spirit this faith
is sealed, as if in the safest of documents, in all those
who let themselves be informed of the truth through
God's Word and believe in the kingdom of God.
The Spirit of Jesus Christ is the only certainty of the
kingdom of God: this is the meaning of the saying of
Jesus that no one can enter the kingdom – no eye can
catch the smallest glimpse of it – unless he is born
again in word and baptism and through the Holy   John 3:3–5
Spirit from above.

It is the Spirit that makes alive; through him,
we are engrafted into the divine nature. All who   2 Pet. 1:4
belong to God's covenant and who are to inherit his
kingdom are transplanted by the Spirit into God's
nature. He makes God's Word true in and through
them. All the promises of the living God find their
yes and amen in him. The Holy Spirit accomplishes   2 Cor. 1:20
all that God wills in those who receive him with joy
and delight. He brings forth the joy that seeks out
and loves all that is God's Word and God's work. The
believing church finds God at work in her midst in
power and in truth, purifying hearts and whole lives
for his will. The Spirit implants what is true and
good, what is just and holy. Under his protection it   Rom. 12:11–21
shall take root, grow, and bear fruit.

For this reason, everything in our nature that
prevents what he has planted from growing must, like

weeds, be suppressed and killed and rooted out by the
Spirit. He does not only abolish evildoing; he takes
away desiring it. Under the influence of the Holy
Spirit, the old man dies, and the new man starts to
live in his place. The law of the Spirit, the law of life,
annuls the law of sin and death through baptism by
the Spirit. The Spirit himself does these works; everything is inspired by him, prompted by him, and urged
on to new life by him. A new creation has arisen – a
new planting, a new birth!

We must be reborn through the Spirit
This re-creation and purification, this rebirth and
renewal, take place as baptism in the stream of the
Titus 3:5–7   Spirit poured out over the church in Jesus Christ.
The covenant of the Holy Spirit, as a matter of divine
birth, is the promise of the freedom of sonship. By
virtue of this birth and impelled by the Holy Spirit,
we live in the covenant of sonship. Only the Spirit
creates children of God. His impelling power is proof
of sonship and its freedom.

    As far as God is concerned, flesh and blood have
1 Cor. 15:50   nothing in common with birth through the Spirit.
The Holy Spirit has an abhorrence of all unfaithful
idolatry and false appearances. He withdraws forever
in the face of the demonic lack of discernment in
any religious mishmash. He disappears where man's
own greatness takes over, where sin gains authority
in opposition to God. With this, every possibility
of sonship and of being a Christian is blotted out.
Whoever lacks the Spirit of Christ does not belong
to him. Human nature and God's nature are opposed
to each other. Where flesh and blood are allowed to

dominate, God must keep his Spirit away and refuse to recognize any sonship.

All children of God bear his living breath as a birthmark showing their genuineness and revealing their origin. God never allows children of evil to be passed off onto him. He acknowledges no spiritual bastards. The Spirit alone, with his inspiration and his lordship, reflects the image of God. He alone is genuine, everything else is deception. The nature and character of God is revealed in his children by the purity of their breath. Only God's Spirit has this purity. Where the truthful and genuine nature of a child of God is found, it governs the whole of life and gives it shape according to the image of God. Genuine truth is God himself; his sons and daughters bear his image and show it forth as their light as long as they allow themselves to be ruled and led in all things by his Spirit. They are his heirs in the Spirit alone – God never denies his own nature.

Gal. 3:26–27

Matt. 5:8

The divine nature becomes truly and effectively rooted in those born a second time, replacing the carnal nature that used to exist in their soul and blood. As a result, with this divine Spirit, the completely different and entirely new life of the kingdom of God is given to them. The Holy Spirit is the first witness to the last kingdom. It is he who establishes living community with God and causes it to begin in truth and deed. It is he who brings the divine nature of the kingdom of God into the believing church. It is this Spirit who assures the church of Jesus Christ that her members are God's heirs. Like a royal anointing in the final kingdom, the pouring-out of the Holy Spirit belongs to baptism in the name of the coming king.

Gal. 5:16–18, 25

Pentecost brought God's kingdom

The so-called baptism of a person who has not
perceived anything of this Spirit can have no validity
for Christ even if it pointed toward him, as baptism
by John the Baptist did. It was baptism in the name
of Jesus Christ that Peter held in readiness for all
those prepared for a change of spirit in their hearts
and lives to be made ready for the kingdom of God.
He promised they would receive the gift of the Holy
Spirit at baptism. What had happened? The king
crowned with the Spirit had been killed and had risen
from his grave! After these earthshaking events, the
reality of the outpouring of God's Spirit heralded the
breaking-in of God's kingdom as promised by the
prophets. This was the content of the Pentecostal
address: The one who has arisen and been glorified
has received the Holy Spirit from the Father. Now
he has poured it out: you can see it; you can hear it.
The Jesus you have executed is the Messiah-King of
God's kingdom. Now at last he pours the Spirit of
his kingdom over all flesh! The Spirit is there! The
kingdom breaks in!

The world-shaking question of the people at
Pentecost – what they should do in the face of this
overwhelming fact – led to Christ and his kingdom.
The forgiveness of sins that prepares the way for the
kingdom culminates in a longing for the Holy Spirit,
that through him it would be possible to lead a life
worthy of God's kingdom. That question concern-
ing Jesus Christ and the kingdom of God resulted
in a readiness for the Holy Spirit, for Jesus Christ
can never be separated from his Spirit. The early
Christian gospel of the forgiveness of sins cannot be

Acts 19:1–7

Acts 2
1 Pet. 3:21

separated from an apostolic life in the Holy Spirit.
The church of Jesus Christ cannot be severed from
the kingdom of God.

The king of God's kingdom, as the Spirit of holy
unity, is the sap of life that brings unity to the living
organism called the church. From Christ as its root,
the Holy Spirit rises into its branches and vines and
makes of the believing church a single, undivided
plant in God's kingdom, an integrated growth that is
one with the crowned king. Christ is God's vine; the
believers are his branches. The Spirit, as the sap, rises
from the roots and fills the branches; he makes them
fruitful and keeps them alive for the kingdom of God.

Isa. 11:1–2
John 15:4–5

As inseparable as fire, heat, and light

At the first full experience of Pentecost, from the one
who had died and risen again, the life of the Spirit
broke in as the coming of the kingdom. The open
tomb proves that it is God's will to rule through the
Spirit of the Risen One. Jakob Böhme bears witness to
it in his own imagery:

> Just as a candle is consumed by fire and, out of that
> very dying, light and strength go forth as powerful
> life, so should and must the eternal, divine sun rise
> out of Christ's dying, out of his death! When Christ
> arises, when the sun comes up, night is swallowed
> up by day and there is no night anymore. So it is with
> the forgiveness of sins.[5]

Out of the wellspring of Jesus Christ, out of the
power of his resurrection, the forgiving Spirit of the
Crucified One flooded over the people at Pentecost.

---

5 Jakob Böhme in Wiesenhütter, *Morgenröte*, 202.

The Word broke forth. All divine spirits and powers were set on fire.

> Just as breath lends voice to the word and gives it shape and sound, so also the breath, wind, and Spirit of God make the Word alive and active within us and lead us into all truth. This is the power of God, doing, working, and perfecting everything; establishing it all; uniting, comforting, teaching, and instructing. All of the Spirit's work in us assures us that we are God's children.[6]

John 16:13

Rom. 8:14

Thus Peter Riedemann, in his *Confession of Faith*, written around the year 1540 on behalf of all the brothers called Hutterian, attests to the unity of the Father and the Son in the Holy Spirit which was a fact at Pentecost.

> When a word is spoken, a breath is exhaled. From both the speaker and the spoken word, a living breath or wind blows, and the sound of a voice goes forth. In the same way the Holy Spirit comes from the Father and the Son, or from the Truth and the Word. Just as the Son or the Word proceeds from the Father and yet remains in him, so the Holy Spirit proceeds from both and remains in both for ever and ever.
>
> . . . Just as fire, heat, and light do not separate from each other (for where one is, there are all three; and where one is lacking, none is present), so it is with the Father, Son, and Holy Spirit. Where one of them is, there are all three; but whoever lacks one lacks all three. One cannot take heat and light away from fire and still have fire. Much less can one take the Son and the Holy Spirit from the Father.[7]

---

6 *Peter Riedemann's Hutterite Confession of Faith*, 76.

7 *Peter Riedemann's Hutterite Confession of Faith*, 75–76.

So the great movement toward brotherhood throughout all centuries, a continually renewed Pentecost, has witnessed vigorously to unity in God. God is unity. Only those who remain in unity remain in God and God in them. The same recognition that dawned on Peter Riedemann came to Jakob Böhme, the other Silesian cobbler, eighty years later:

1 John 4:16

> The eternal Word of the Father, which is the very heart of the Father, is born out of the wrath of darkness through the fire of the Father. Through fire, he reveals himself in the light as one single being with three characteristics: as the Father like the world of fire; as the Son like the world of light – like the love-longing that is in light; and as the Holy Spirit like stirring life.
>
> The eternal Father is revealed in fire in its entirety; the Son in the light of fire; and the Holy Spirit in the power of life and movement in the light of the kingdom of joy, as the power streaming forth from the flame of love! Imagine, then, that the Father is the fire of the celestial bodies; that the Son is his heart as the sun, which bathes them all in blissful light; and that the Holy Spirit is the breath of life, without which there could be no sun and no stars.[8]

Perfect unity in God is the spiritual reality of his love within himself, to be comprehended only in the very center of his heart. Only by the central fire of his love can God in his unity be known; he cannot be recognized by the nature of the first creation, nor by its wrathful fire of judgment, nor by its laws (necessary in the coercive rule of governments). The central

---

8 Jakob Böhme in Wiesenhütter, *Morgenröte*, 118–119.

light of God's heart has been revealed in Jesus. The Son, as an independent person, yet in the Father, is the inmost depths of the Father's heart. Jesus Christ is the loving center of the heart of God from which proceed the all-compelling powers of the Holy Spirit.

John 3:16

In the Spirit of Jesus Christ, the Father's heart as the joy of perfect love comes down to a love-impoverished earth that is shaking in the judgment of God's wrath. In Christ, God's heart comes as the Holy Spirit to people who had become estranged from God's love. In this Spirit the church is created, whose unity is God's unity. The king of the kingdom of God is the Spirit of the church. His church knows no other commission than peace and unity. She is charged with the commission of love and justice, which is the heart of God's kingdom. The only thing at work in her is the radiant glory of the eternal power of love proceeding from Christ.

Eph. 2:18–22

The one who has gone out from the heart of God and has been exalted to become ruler of God's kingdom is at the same time the Spirit of the church. Here he brings about the transformation of the believers into light, so that from now on the representation of his coming kingdom is laid upon them in the power of this Spirit of love. Where the heart of God's love prevails, the Spirit of Jesus Christ rules. But where the thoughts and deeds of hot-blooded people have broken with the heart of God in anger (however justified), where they have broken with Christ's nature of love, his Holy Spirit retreats, filled with indignation and aversion. It was the same when the Law with its bloody sentences was first introduced and when human monarchy first arose in Israel. The Spirit calls for God. The Spirit of

Jesus Christ flees from human greatness and power.   Luke 18:9–17
He seeks the humble, those with a childlike spirit. In   Matt. 5:3
them he glorifies the inmost heart of God.

Only in Christ, in the perfect love of God's heart,
only in the way that leads to the cross, does God show
his unity through the Holy Spirit. Without Christ and
his way, without apostolic poverty in absolute simplicity and dedication, without a love that has nothing
to do with rights or violence, people will always be far
from the kingdom of God and far from the workings
of his Spirit in the church. Only those who abide in
God and God in them live in the unity of a love that
sacrifices everything. Ulrich Stadler, a coworker of
Jakob Hutter and Peter Riedemann, witnessed to this
truth with these authoritative words:

> Whoever does not follow Christ on his way and walk
> in his footsteps, whoever is unwilling to carry his
> cross, does not have or know the Son; and whoever
> does not have the Son does not know the Father; nor
> can he be enlightened through the loving-kindness
> of the Holy Spirit. It is into Christ, who dwells in us,
> that we must be incorporated in order to become
> partakers of the one Trinity through the solemn
> justice of the cross of Christ. Through this we
> become incorporated in the body of Christ, of which
> Christ is the head.[9]

The church of his Holy Spirit, as the body of Christ,
is the only place on earth where the unity of God
is revealed in Christ, that is, in the Holy Spirit. The
nature of God is shown so clearly and unitedly here
that his one will is done on earth. His kingdom comes

---

9 Ulrich Stadler, died 1540, quoted from an old Hutterian "epistle book"
given to Arnold by Hutterites in Manitoba, Canada.

to us as the unity of the church. Here the way of
Jesus is followed to the end – death on the cross in
the name of love. Here men receive the Holy Spirit
as community with God in Christ. Ulrich Stadler
continues:

Here first of all, and nowhere else, grows true knowledge of the Father in the Son, so that we abide in him
and he in us, so that in the Holy Spirit we are the one

Eph. 4:2–6   body of Jesus Christ the crucified. . . . Everywhere,
Christ shows the strict justice and righteousness of
the Father. The Father carries it out in Christ, and
it is put into practice by all who wish to grow and
increase in the body of Christ, whereby the Son of
God can be recognized.

God cannot forsake those who are spiritually
poor, who hunger and thirst after righteousness;
he will feed them through the Spirit with his body

Matt. 5:6   of unity. They must thereby be transformed into
the community of Christ's body. To such shall be
revealed the third part in God: the loving-kindness
and mercy of the Holy Spirit. Such people do not live
for themselves, however, but for Christ in them, and
they are therefore glad and joyful in the Holy Spirit,
through whom they truly know the Father, the Son,
and the Holy Spirit.

What then do they actually see through the Holy
Spirit? The Father in the power of his omnipotence,
by whom they were created; they see and know the
Son in whom they are tested, purified, justified,
and circumcised, in whom they have truly become
children of God. Therefore they have free access to
the Father and are now one with Christ and all their
fellow members: they are all one church and one

body in Christ. They are in the kingdom of God and have Christ as their Lord. In this unity, everything is held in common; nothing is privately owned. Here it comes to pass that the Lord pours out his Spirit over all flesh, and all are taught by God to live to all eternity according to his will, filled with all good things.

The whole community of the Hutterian brothers bears witness with Ulrich Stadler in all these things. They maintain that the indivisible unity of the church was first created in Jerusalem in the outpouring of the Holy Spirit. As a revelation of this Spirit, she shows in her life and work the perfect unity of the eternal will of God – and his coming rulership – with the way of Jesus Christ. That God is in himself indivisibly united (as the Father with the Son in the Spirit) is revealed today in the complete unity of the church, and here alone – until at the end of time the kingdom of God will spread the rule of his unity over   John 17:20–21 the whole world.

The first church was a community

The Pentecostal spring of the first Christian church contrasts sharply with the icy rigidity of our Christianity today. Everyone senses that at that time a fresher wind blew and purer water flowed, a stronger power and a more fiery warmth ruled than is the case today among all those who call themselves Christians. We all know that in spite of the different churches, in spite of all the various religious alliances and societies for moral edification, the community life of faith and love represented by the early church is almost not to be found today. What has Christianity in general lost? What was the all-important event that took place in Jerusalem? The word of Jesus, and even more, his life and deeds from the manger to the cross, were alive and present in that first circle of the Christ-movement. What the apostles had to say and do was drawn directly from the same reality that comes to meet us today in the four Gospels. This community of faith and community of life in the first love was marked by the presence of Christ – the Christ who had said, "I am with you always."

Matt. 28:20

Jesus devoted himself to people's outer need just as much as to their inner need, demonstrating the cleansing and healing power of the kingdom of God wherever he went. It was the same in the early church. It is not true that Jesus' Christianity is exclusively concerned with souls, despising our bodies as our lot in life and as a purely outward matter. When Jesus cast out all the demonic spirits through the Spirit of God, the kingdom of God came to us. When one of the finest of men sent and asked Jesus whether it was he who would bring in the future state of justice, or whether they should wait for another, he answered by referring to his deeds: in his presence sick bodies were healed and the dead brought to life. Tidings of joy were brought to the poor. "Come! See!" was his summons.

Matt. 12:28

Matt. 11:2–5

In Jesus' presence, the invisible kingdom of God had become visible reality; the Word had taken shape, and the meaning of love had become real. His word and life had proved that love knows no bounds. Love halts at no barrier and can never be stopped, no matter where or under what circumstances it seems impossible to practice love. Nothing is impossible for the faith that springs from love. For this reason, the

1 Cor. 13:4–5

call of Jesus did not stop at property. When he felt a love for the young man who was rich in possessions, he looked into his heart and said the word of perfect love, "One thing is still lacking: sell everything you have; give it to the poor and come follow me." Matt. 19:16–22

Yet what gave his friends strength to put into practice the will to love, as he himself had instilled it into them, was the experience of the Spirit. When this Spirit was given by the Risen One to the new church-to-be, he overturned everything and set it on fire. Then they were able to become a life-sharing community, and only then did their love as unity in the Holy Spirit overflow. They were all on fire with the same burning love, which drew them irresistibly and for always together. Love had become in them a holy "thou must." Just as Jesus had always wanted round him his nearest friends and pupils, whom we call disciples, so his Spirit drew the early Christians close to one another. Together they felt compelled to live the life of Jesus, and together, in complete community, they had to do the same as he had done. Because they felt this absolute, inner must, all questions concerned with living together found an answer that accorded completely with the perfect unity and purity of love.

Jesus summoned each individual to leave everything and be with him wherever he went. He traveled Matt. 4:18–22 from village to village with the band he had called together, and whatever their daily experiences were, they shared them in common. In accordance with the will of the leader, a common purse was kept. Yet his mission was never meant to be limited to a narrow circle. The band of itinerant followers of Jesus became his embassy. The twelve apostles expected and represented his kingdom of justice as the approaching brotherhood in God. The resurrection confirmed the power of this mission. As soon as the Spirit of Jesus flooded so unhindered over his first church, its first outward form was bound to take shape according to the way of Jesus and the commission entrusted to his embassy. The early Christians held absolutely everything in common. Whoever had possessions was filled with the urge to share them. No one had anything that did not belong to the community. By this time, through the exuberant and united life of the Holy Spirit, a bigger group had grown together to unity in God on the way of Jesus Christ.

Matt. 10

Acts 5:14

This could not be an exclusive unity: all living things grow. Life begets life and spreads. Perfect love never remains exclusive. Open doors and open hearts were significant characteristics of the early Christians, who therefore had access to everyone and gained the love of whole peoples. They were a light that shone for all. The fiery Spirit who filled them wanted to pour himself out over all flesh as God's will for his empire: the Spirit of God's kingdom wants to be victorious over all peoples to draw them together as one. In this Spirit, the early church was burning and alive, all heart and all soul; only in this could so many become one heart and one soul. Not the hard light of cold intellectual knowledge was to be found here but the illuminating Spirit, who sets the heart aglow and quickens the soul with burning, fiery love.

Act 2:39

Only in this way could the ice-cold existence of isolation be overcome. Communal life with its white-hot love began. In its heat, property was melted away to the very foundations. The icy substructures

of age-old glaciers melt before God's sun. The only
way to abolish private property and personal assets is
through the radiant power of the life-creating Spirit.
All ownership feeds on stifling self-interest. When
deadly selfishness is killed by love, and only then,
ownership comes to an end. Yet it was so in the early
church: under the influence of the Spirit of commu-
nity, no one thought his goods were his own. Private   Acts 4:32
property was an impossibility; here the Spirit of love
and unity ruled.

Love overlooks no need or suffering. In such a
life-sharing community no one could suffer a lack of
clothing, food, or any other necessity of life. Whoever
wants to keep goods and valuables for himself in spite
of the need around him must have done violence
to his own heart. God's heart is never limited in
its sphere of action. Those who held their goods in
common at Jerusalem gave generous hospitality to
thousands of pilgrims. Through the Spirit poured out
upon them, they were able to care wisely for many,
for very many, with the slenderest means; soon the
early church experienced the dutiful support of her
apostolic daughter churches in this enormous service.

The Spirit is sensitive

The early church had an immeasurable effect far
and wide. It shook whole worlds; it established a
completely different and undreamed-of new world.
But the Spirit burning with love is more delicate
than the hard edifices of calculating reason and its
coldly organizing social structure; more delicate also
than the powers of the soul and the blood, which so
many extended families and national communities
try to use as a foundation. Because the Holy Spirit

is supremely noble and supremely divine, he is more sensitive than all other forms of life when he is confronted with anything coarse or gross. Free from all connection with other elements, he drives them all away, or he withdraws before they can offend him.

The Spirit alone is inviolable. He is the most delicate element of all. The all-pervading celestial ether never forces itself on crude, earthy matter. On earth what lasts longest belongs to the realm of the crudest. The finer the organs, the more endangered is their life. The kingdom Jesus brought, which has to do with the pure Spirit, is not of this gross world. Unless this world is smelted and remolded, his Spirit cannot touch it. The Spirit of Jesus broke into a world grown alien to him and overcame all other powers as the mightier one, who is and always will be inviolably pure. He cannot deny his nature. He never becomes part of any mixture. He cannot and will not let himself be changed by anything alien to him.

The Spirit is alive as the power of love at work without violence, as an inner voice of the utmost delicacy. He is perceived with the inner eye of pure faith alone. He retreats when the inner vision is not concentrated on him alone, when other spirits are given room beside him. He would rather see a Spirit-filled witness murdered than allow alien and violent spirits to gain room beside him. What if this earthly life is taken from those who confess him? What does it matter? He himself cannot be killed; he is invincible. He rules forever, but he does not impose his rule on any opponent: he seems to flee from a gross and violent world. His church must suffer the same fate as Christ on the cross. Like Jesus himself,

John 18:36

the early church could light up the new way only as a
short flash of eternal clarity.

Phil. 2:14–16

It almost seemed as if the form of life brought
about by the Spirit of Pentecost fled forever from this
world with its extermination at the second destruction of Jerusalem. Yet throughout the centuries, we
see the same perfect form given by the same Spirit
again and again like a very rare gift of God. In fact
it never has fled from this earth. But just as each
individual filled with the Spirit has only a limited
span of life in this time-bound world, so the pure
form in which the church took shape has been wiped
out again and again by violent enemies. Individual
churches were brought to a bloody end. Witnesses
were slain. Yet the Spirit remained alive. Like Jesus
and like the apostles, the early church and the subse-
quent churches of the Reformation were also allotted
a very limited time on this blood-drenched earth.

Yet new children are continually being born to the
Spirit. The gaps made by death are filled by newly
engendered life. As more are murdered, more follow
on. The blood of martyrs is always the seed of the
church. The living seed grain is always the mystery
of the church and the kingdom. It would be entirely

Matt. 13:31

wrong to force an imitation of the form of life this
mystery takes; such efforts can only lead to a lifeless caricature without the one essential element:
the freely moving Spirit, the life born of God! One
thing alone matters: to become open to the living
God, to the life-giving Spirit of Jesus Christ, so that
he – and he alone – can bring into being the same
life he gave the early Christians. Then new life-units
will constantly arise, in which the love that comes

to expression in full community encompasses and penetrates everything. Full community is a question of rebirth and resurrection. It has been given even in our times by the Spirit of Jesus Christ, in the power of eternal birth and continual resurrection.

The essence of the Holy Spirit is unity

The one decisive thing is the Spirit in which that unique circle, the early church, lived – the quickening Spirit that alone decided everything. It is a matter of recognizing the working of the Spirit and how strong and pure it is. Spirit! Who is he? And what does he do? The very essence of the Spirit is unity. His love is born of that joy which pours out of the heart of God. Where people have to be disciplined or even forced, the Spirit of love retreats, taking with him the unity of life he brings. Unity cannot be "made." Joy and love cannot be forced. It was the free and living Spirit of joy that filled those people with the urge to be together daily and for always in love, in the bright radiance of community in God. His Spirit of unity, love, and joy made community of goods and work inevitable.

There was no class hatred there; no sinister ferocity coming from a joyless, demanding power; no hint of bitterness, the result of disappointed claims; no talk of demanding human rights whereby, even as a man looks after others, he wants to look after himself and his own. The free impulse to give away wealth was alive there: the believers wanted to give themselves to the cause with all they had and all they could do. The mystery of this early church is revealed in the fact that here the Spirit of Jesus Christ has disclosed God's heart. The most profound heart of all gives itself. In the church is revealed the creative spirit of a love that never fails.

In the name and reality of Jesus, a believing circle had gathered around the heart of God, a church that made God's perfect love clear and recognizable by her complete unity. God had formed an organism and the apostle was given the decisive word for it: "the body of Christ." It is the second and new embodiment of love and the Word. The Word goes forth from the heart of the Father through the life-giving and uniting Spirit. Christ is the Word, which takes shape anew when believing people live in full community. The Word becomes the church.

Eph. 4:4, 12, 16

1 Cor. 12

The Holy Spirit can reveal himself only as the spirit he is: the spirit of *unity*. All members of the one body are filled with the same Spirit streaming through them, and thus they know they are united as one organism. The life of the believing church is unity and community in the Holy Spirit, characteristic of the church endowed with his gifts. She proves it through the organic working together of all her diverse powers. When these powers of the unifying Spirit work together creatively, the constructive peace of the church and of the coming kingdom comes into being and forms a firm bond.

The church is a reality only insofar as her structure corresponds to the glad tidings of the all-embracing kingdom. As one heart and one soul, she must stand united for the inviolability of God's peace. In the brotherliness of the uniting Spirit and as the mission of the kingdom of God, she must fight in faith for God's justice to conquer the whole world.

The church is able to hold out until this last battle,
for she is united, and God is her strength. In harmony
and unanimity, she unites all her members in the
same love for the same task.

Rom. 15:5–7
Phil. 2:1–4

In the power and authority of the Holy Spirit, the
community of the whole church is of one heart and
mind, united in faith and common expectation for
God's whole universe. From this crowning unity,
her unfeigned love and all-embracing faith long to
put everything to the service of God. She wants to
summon all the nations of the world to partake in
God's kingdom. Where God gives the courage of
faith, where Christ's mission lives as community,
the love that comes from God's Spirit proves to be a
power that subjects all things to the rulership of God.

2 Cor. 5:20

The Spirit leads the church into mission

In the power of the Holy Spirit, joy in the kingdom
of God will show itself in every situation as absolute
certainty. It never draws back in dismay from any
ruling power, however widely recognized. The
supreme justice of God's constructive peace should
alone prevail! Love arises from it and out of love arise
joy and faith as fruits of the Spirit. What grows out
of the Holy Spirit has divine strength and knows no
limits: a courageous assurance of victory fills the
whole church with militancy. With exultant joy in
the Holy Spirit, she takes up what is humanly impossible – the word of omnipotent authority. This affects
everything and applies to everybody as does the
overwhelming certainty of the believing church about
the future.

Eph. 6:10–17

Equipped with the courage of the Holy Spirit, the
church dares to do spiritual battle with all powers

that withstand her love. All resistance of the present
age is insignificant in her eyes. The Spirit who guides
and instructs her is himself the utmost encourage-
ment. He sends out a summons to take up the cause,
the cause that matters more than anything else! As
its appointed representative, he is the administrator
and advocate, interceding everywhere for the church.   John 15:26
He leads her in battle. He tells her what to say. He fills
her with courage to represent his mission resolutely
in the most dangerous situations. The members of
the church become his organs, for he pours the love
of God into their hearts. He uses the church in word
and in work as the instrument of his inmost will.

The church receives a royal promise especially
meant for the dangers of persecution: the Spirit of
the all-commanding Father will go with his sons and
daughters to speak to his enemies through them. He
will instruct them at every decisive moment. Under
his leadership, they will be masters of any situation
until the last hour comes. He puts into their hearts
what they have to do and suffer, what they have to say
and be responsible for. They are filled with the Holy
Spirit, ardently longing for the final revelation. In the
face of death, they proclaim and represent the eternal
truth as it is given to them by the Holy Spirit, who
prompts them, moves them, and impels them. So to
their last breath they give witness to Jesus, that he is
the Messiah-King of the long-promised kingdom.   Acts 7:54–56

Through the Spirit sent from heaven, everything
the prophets attested about the kingdom of God is
brought to all people by the long-suffering church.
Those prophets, as holy men of God, acted in all they
did according to the promptings of the Holy Spirit.

In the same way, the commission and authority of the kingdom is now entrusted to those sent out by the church. When the Spirit himself speaks in the apostles as he did in the prophets, they utter his word. The apostolic Spirit is the prophetic Spirit: his word is his kingdom. The apostolic mission is a matter of the prophetic embassy of God, which brings the future kingdom to all people here and now. As prophecy, the apostleship of the church embraces the whole truth of Jesus and his future, from the widest perspective down to its smallest fulfillment.

The Holy Spirit determines where those on this mission should go and what they should say: the Spirit speaking within them tells them which people they should speak to, which land they should go to or avoid. The Spirit's guidance gives final certainty. Under his leadership, no matter what it points to, fear is unknown. Often he leads into the midst of the plain of death, making the downfall of humankind horribly clear; at decisive moments in history, the Spirit leads people into extreme danger in the wilderness, where they are tempted by the devil. Yet everywhere he demonstrates the triumphant reality of the resurrection: victory over the temptations of hell.

Ezek. 37:1

1 Cor. 15:54–57

To venture anything with the Spirit is more serious than death, more powerful than when all the hosts of God draw near with overwhelming power. He strikes people like lightning. As the strong one, he overpowers the weak. Those who receive him are thrown to the ground and put on their feet again, made new. The strong one remains over them and dwells in them. The weak body becomes the dwelling of the strong Spirit: for the church, as the body of

Jer. 20:7

Rev. 1:16–17

Acts 9:1–9

Christ, is the temple of the Holy Spirit, and all those
who receive the Spirit belong to her. All believers are
living members of the church, pervaded by the Spirit,
which fills her whole body. Like Gideon, the church
wears the armor of the Spirit over her whole body.

Judg. 6:12

The Holy Spirit fills the church

From the very beginning, the Holy Spirit has filled
everything belonging to the church, even the
preparation of the way for her: the last prophet of
olden times, who preceded the coming Christ, was
filled with him while still in his mother's womb; his
father and mother had become full of the Holy Spirit   Luke 1:41, 67
for him; before Jesus' life began, Mary received the
Spirit; and from the time the apostolic church began   Luke 1:35
to follow Jesus Christ, it was filled with the Holy
Spirit. "When they had prayed, the place where they
were gathered was shaken, and they were all filled
with the Holy Spirit and spoke the Word of God with
joyful courage."   Acts 4:31

Whoever came within the church's domain
received the Holy Spirit. The "servants of temporal
needs," those who in this community of love were
responsible for administering economic and social
justice, also had to be full of the Holy Spirit like the
apostles. Their work, as a concern of the church,   Acts 6:3
was to be filled with the Spirit's divine wisdom, as is
testified of Stephen (the first to do this service), that
until the last moment of his martyrdom he was filled
with the Holy Spirit. What was true of him was true
of all: even Paul, the latecomer among the apostles,
like all the other serving members of the church, was
filled with the Holy Spirit as soon as the blindness

inflicted by the lightning of the Spirit was taken away from him.

Acts 9:17–19

God gives his strong Spirit to the whole church; he fills her entirely. In her body he lets the complete image of Jesus Christ shine out. He penetrates every area of her life with certain knowledge of what sin, justice, and judgment are; what faith and love are; and what work it is that Christ has accomplished and how it can be done through him alone. The Spirit of Jesus Christ wants to reach and convict each member of the church, teaching and educating him.

John 16:8–11

The Spirit is given to all believers – it is imparted by God to each member united with his church. He wants to make all of them people of faith, whose united action makes the justice of Jesus a reality. It is God whom the whole church calls upon, God who does everything connected with Christ's cause, God's works that are done when the unity of the believers calls for them to be done. God is the one who acts. He acts through the Holy Spirit by virtue of the apostolic gospel of Jesus Christ.

The church's unity of action springs from its community with the Father of Jesus Christ. It is founded on the teaching of the apostles, on their spirit, word, and life. It is alive in prayer to God in the name of Jesus Christ. Without the apostolic Spirit and without his teaching and community, no Christian can draw near to God, and there is no Christian prayer. Only in the authority of the Spirit can God be called upon: God shall intervene. His unity shall shine out, and his kingdom shall draw near. His will shall be done, and his nature shall be revealed. His forgiveness shall take effect, and his omnipotence

John 16:23–24

1 Cor. 12:3

shall break the power of evil. He shall give bread and
life. He shall be victorious over the hour of tempta-
tion every time it comes over the earth. It is God who   Matt. 6:9–15
wills and accomplishes everything, but it can happen
only through the call of the apostolic Spirit of Jesus
Christ, who is the Spirit of God.

When in our human weakness we are at a loss to
know how to stand before God in his omnipotence,
when we cannot see how our pleading is to count
for anything before Christ and his rulership, it is the
Spirit alone who comes to the aid of our weakness.
We of ourselves do not know what to pray for. Our
manner of praying does not in the least correspond to
what is fitting before God; but the Spirit himself represents the believers powerfully with cries that soar
up, cries we are unable to utter; the one who searches   Rom. 8:25–27
hearts knows what the Spirit has in mind: the Spirit
wants and does what God wants and does. He is one   1 Cor. 2:10–12
with God. He sanctifies the unholy and represents
them as holy in those things that please God.

God wants to be honored through this one Spirit
alone. The church, gathered in silence, waits for the
Spirit's prompting; if people want to learn from him,
they must be able to listen to him. It is those who   1 Sam. 3:7–9
listen whom he wants to teach. He is their Master.
He wants them to call upon God in such a way that
the listener becomes the speaker and the speaker, the
listener. Thus God listens to believers; because he
hears them, his Spirit and the Spirit's cause will be
theirs, just as they have requested. This is the only
way of speaking with God. All other so-called prayer
is an abomination to God. Whoever turns his ear
away so that he cannot hear God's voice prays in vain:

God rejects his prayer. Whoever wants to combine other plans with what God has in mind fails to meet God. Whoever gets diverted loses the way. Whoever is divided remains far from God. Whoever wants to appear in God's presence with a double heart will not gain from him anything of Christ.

Luke 9:62

The Holy Spirit is a spirit of reverence. The holiest things, such as calling on God in the name of Jesus Christ, can be dared only through the prompting of the one Holy Spirit and only when all human wishes are completely silenced. Christians remain human and do not become gods; their own and other spirits never stop harassing and oppressing the new life given them. For this reason they are in continual need of the unchangeable Spirit. They must pray daily that he move and fill their hearts anew. It is certain that God hears them and gives his Holy Spirit to all who call upon him in dedicated reverence and expectant faith.

Matt. 7:7

The Holy Spirit is indivisible

God gives his Spirit wholly. God cannot mete out his greatest gift with weights and measures – it is not a substance that can be divided. The Spirit is the living God himself; as the Father and the Son are. The three are one, they are God. The indivisible one gives himself in all his fullness to those ready to obey him. Where he can act and work as he wills, he gives himself wholly and remains the one he was and always will be. He never contradicts himself: he says the same to all believers. He wants to lead all of them into the complete truth without withholding anything: he has no intention of giving them half-truths.

John 15:7

John 16:13

He is the whole truth of God, as the Father has revealed it for all time in Christ.

It is God's will, through the power of his Spirit, to fulfill every word spoken by Jesus. It is God's purpose, through the church of his Spirit, to accomplish once more the perfect works of Jesus Christ. He lays the fullness of the Spirit on the whole church of Jesus Christ; with her, he wants to make his history among us: the history of his heart as the history of Jesus Christ. The history of the church is the history of God. The history of the last times, of his kingdom, is present reality in the church. Whoever despises the representatives of the church despises not people but God, who has entrusted to the church of his Spirit the task of representing his holy cause. God's administrator, the representative of Jesus Christ, is the advocate of the church. Zech. 12:10

The Spirit is the sign by which the church can be recognized and known as belonging to the kingdom of God. By the Holy Spirit she knows she remains in Christ. God, as the Spirit of his kingdom, is in the church of Jesus Christ: the invisible Spirit is unmistakable. He is the Spirit of the Father, whose heart of perfect love is a present reality. He is the Spirit of the Son! The unmistakable word and nature of Jesus Christ, his perfect act of sacrifice, and his future are revealed in the Spirit. Isa. 61:1

The Holy Spirit is not a spirit of the times

The Holy Spirit is a spirit of counsel and wisdom. Through the life of Jesus, he makes God's will known in all events and situations. God and his wisdom, Jesus and his counsel never become reality outside Isa. 11:2

the province of the Spirit. In work and in life it becomes clear that without the Spirit of new life and new works people can know neither the Father nor the Son, however wisely they talk or write about the highest things with human knowledge.

John 5:19 The work of the Spirit honors no one but God. Everything he does contrasts the greatness of God with the smallness of man and proves everywhere that God's kingdom is completely different from our 1 John 3:20 world. God's heart is greater than our hearts. God's Spirit is absolutely different from the spirit of man: the divine power of the Holy Spirit can be recognized 2 Cor. 12:9–10 in contrast to human weakness. Like water on parched land, the Spirit is poured out over ignorant and feeble people: this quite other Spirit of God's free heights pours over the lowest and most enslaved.

The Spirit reveals God's cause as a bounteous and undeserved gift, as a grace descending directly from Acts 10:44 above, as the actual fact of a direct pouring-in. God's Spirit is the grace of Jesus Christ. Nothing in those who receive the Spirit could possibly justify a claim that the Spirit belongs by rights to them. The Spirit of the heights comes to the undeserving and unworthy, a grace given to those who are humble.

The Spirit of God never grows out of the zeitgeist. In all the human aberrations of today, he proves that his divine character belongs to the ultimate future. God's Spirit never grows out of human works. He comes from another world. Like a heavenly dove, he comes from above to those who are below. He is the Spirit of a kingdom ruling in God's heavens, and from here alone he comes to the earth. As the Spirit of prophetic speech, he turns all eyes to the last things,

to all things that through God shall be brought to
pass at the end of days.

In contrast to the zeitgeist of any human epoch,
the Spirit is always untimely, pointing ultimately to
the world peace of the future. His knowledge runs
ahead of all contemporary history. He belongs to no
earthly kingdom. Every state and nation looks upon
him as alien; everywhere, he is the different spirit.
He reveals a divine justice that can be expected
only from afar. His rule comes from a world outside
our space. His truth is not to be grasped by human
thinking: God's light from the world beyond gives an
insight that infinitely surpasses all human knowledge
and experience of time and space.

Jesus brought the Spirit of the Creator. Only the
Spirit who himself brought about the creation of all
things can understand them. Only he who sees into
all things and who is still at work today is and always
will be above all that takes place and unfolds in
creation. Only the creative Spirit manifests the power
that is unending and eternal. Only he knows the
depths of the Godhead, for he alone is the living bond
that unites the first creation with the new future, the
final creation. He grants superlative clarity and power
from beyond to the feeblest of creatures: in spite of a
hostile and murderous age and the narrow confines
of space, and in spite of our weakness, we are able to
believe in, and live in keeping with, the kingdom of
heaven and its holy future.

Whoever accepts the Spirit of the new creation
(which brings the end of the old, first creation in its
train) receives the eternal powers of the one God who
formed the first creation in the same Spirit. God's

2 Cor. 5:17

future is alive now as the Spirit of strength in an aging universe wherever people expect the end that will transform everything. The new day has already dawned. All shall see it: a new creation is arising! Its gospel is meant for every creature! The groaning of the old creation meets the sons of the new world.

Mark 16:15

Rom. 8:19–23

An earthly and heavenly church

Heaven's power, as the authority of the Holy Spirit, is at work in a church of the new creation. It lives in her as a living promise of the sunny days to come over an earth that is growing cold. In the midst of an aged world, the church, impregnated with eternity and filled with the future, gains strength for God and his kingdom through the Spirit. The church receives eternal and infinite majesty as a first beam of light from the future. Going forth from the throne of God's rule, the Lord of Light fills the church of the eternal Spirit.

The Holy Spirit descends from the throne of God to a small and weak band gathered in expectant faith to receive him. Faith in the Holy Spirit is faith in the church of light around God's almighty throne. Here the old has passed away. All creatures can see the new creation! Whoever believes in the Holy Spirit has faith in the one Christian church of the kingdom of heaven, which is united and common to all believers, the church of God which as the community of saints has the authority to forgive sins and believes in the resurrection of the body. This faith in the church lives in the realm of the eternal, as revealed by the Spirit.

Matt. 16:19

The sin and death of the old creation must retreat. New life arises, and the church of the Spirit shows the newborn creation. The Holy Spirit and the mother

church giving birth to eternal life are one. From the
city church of the Jerusalem above, the Spirit and
church come down as one. This oneness is what is   Heb. 12:22–23
new in the approaching day of creation. The Spirit of
the church carries the gospel to all creation. In new
birth, he lets his children see the light of day – God's   John 3:1–21
new day.

The church in heaven is the source of all faith
Like Mary the virgin, the church, through the Holy
Spirit, is the eternal mother. Without her there are no
children. Not just any gathering of contemporaries
gives birth to life out of its circle: as far as life *is* there,
it comes from union with a higher unity through
birth in the Spirit. The church takes shape only where
the Holy Spirit has brought about a life and faith
completely at one with the whole glorified band of
martyrs and witnesses, with the apostolic mother
church of all centuries.

The church is built from above. This unity of the
spiritual church around the throne of God is brought
down to the earth by the Holy Spirit. In no other way
or place can church life come into existence, or the
structure of the church be built. The unanimity of
the believing church is in the perfect unity between
her members living now and the one truly united
church of all time. In the Holy Spirit, God's upper
world becomes one with the church on earth. The
secret of the city on the hill is the Spirit. There is
no city below except through the Spirit's one way of
unity with the city above; outside of this there is no
church. God's city-church lives only in the mountain
air of her eternal hill. Her citizenship and her politics
are in heaven. She expects everything from heaven   Matt. 5
and is governed from there.

They will worship in the Spirit and in truth

Through the Spirit of the city of God and only in this one city of the Spirit, worship of God begins; worship in the Spirit and in truth begins in Christ. All other ways of honoring God have come to an end: their places of worship fall into ruins, and their towers are laid low. The houses of God built with stone are done away with – the Spirit is there instead. God does not recognize any church – or congregation or Christian community – unless it is pervaded by the one church that the Holy Spirit, sent by God, establishes and gathers, guides from above, and instructs from the future. Whoever exposes himself to the wind of the Spirit blowing down from above surrenders to the one and only church of Jesus Christ – only in her and going out from her does the Holy Spirit work.

John 4:23–24

The church of Christ is a house of the Holy Spirit and, being built by God, is free of belfries and all the architectural skill of men. In all houses of religious worship built by men, the spirits are mixed. In the house of God there are never many spirits: only one is acknowledged there. No person can stay in this house who does not receive in his or her own heart the one Spirit who fills the whole house. God has built this church for himself. It stands there without manmade towers as the simplest house of God. Like water from the mountains, the Spirit of the heights seeks the lowest place – he wants to go downward. His church bears the lowly and childlike Spirit that alone is of God. The church is with Mary in the stable and comes into being by the side of Christ on the gallows. She goes the way of apostolic poverty. With one heart and one mind, she glorifies no one but God in Christ Jesus.

1 Cor. 3:16

Eph. 2:19–22

All the members of this church, through the
one united Spirit, prove they are Christ's disciples.
In perfect unity of heart and mind, they show the
character of Jesus Christ, unfalsified. He stripped
himself of all greatness and laid aside all privileges; so
does the church. He refused to hold on to anything
that might seem to be his as a special right; so does
the church. It seemed to him like robbery to own
anything that did not also belong to those he loved
from his heart; so it seems to the church. He took the
lowliest place of a hanged slave; so does his church.
All her members deny themselves as he denied
himself. They bear his cross. They are his friends, for
they do what he commands.

Phil. 2:1–16
Matt. 16:24
John 14:21

Jesus' Spirit has called them to his way, to discipleship; he keeps them on it and holds them to it. In
unity with the life of Jesus, they are led in the fight
by his Spirit. With the authoritative word of his
absolute rule, the Spirit of Jesus Christ regulates
everything that takes place among them. On the way
of Jesus Christ no person rules but only the Holy
Spirit, through the power of Christ's sacrificial love.
Unity lives in the readiness for death that comes from
utmost freedom. Here the miracle of the dictatorship
of love comes into being; prompted and guided by
the Spirit, it is a supreme free-willingness, a freedom
whose deepest longing is to sacrifice everything.

1 John 2:27

There is no other church of Jesus Christ than
the one completely free of human authority, built
and directed by the Spirit of Christ's sacrifice. She
remains at one in the Holy Spirit, the one foundation
of truth, the very soul of readiness for the cross. In
the church, the truth of God proves itself to be the

perfect love that comes from the Spirit. The Holy
Spirit continually confirms, fortifies, and purifies
the church, this perfect work of God and of Jesus
Christ's love, completed on the cross. Whoever will-
ingly suffers a renewal of this work in the church and
surrenders to it patiently and serenely, whoever is
prepared to lose his or her life for God's cause as Jesus

Matt. 20:22–23   lost his, is a member of his body. But whoever does
not find the courage and endurance to accept this
work does not belong to the church of Jesus Christ.

The Spirit's emissaries gather people
Only through the Spirit of the Crucified One can this
church that has courage to face death be gathered
and held together. This Spirit is her joy in life and
her inspiration in death. His blazing fire kindles an
enthusiasm for the ultimate sacrifice – all members

Phil. 2:17–18   of the church are ready for it. In a special way, those
called upon to be ready for death in mission must be

Phil. 3:10   invested with a spirit of utmost sacrifice: they must
bear the sword of the Spirit, drive out devils, proclaim
a break with the status quo, spread the victorious
light of God, and scatter the biting salt of truth.
They must call to repentance and faith, represent the
embassy of the city on the hill, and reveal the image
of God. The sign by which they are known is the
community of the cross.

The working of the Holy Spirit for the good is to
be so clearly recognizable in these members of the
church that no one but God can be glorified in everything they say and do. This mission can be given only

2 Cor. 3:5–6   through the power and action of the Spirit, who is not
of man but of God. Christ commanded his disciples
not to stir from their place until they were endued

with power from on high. They were not allowed to Luke 24:49
gather people until they had received the gift of the
Holy Spirit. Without their receiving the Spirit, the
mission of Jesus Christ could never be carried out,
and the disciples could never have become apostles.
Without Christ, who is the Spirit, no apostolic deeds
can be done, and no works can stand before God.

The holiest work of all is the service of apostolic
mission. It may never be undertaken in self-delusion
or human presumption. The truth can be spread
abroad, the word of mission ventured, only according
to the instructions and guidance of the Spirit, that
Spirit who filled Jesus Christ before he was sent by
his Father. How much more does he long that his
messengers never go out on mission except in the
power of this same Spirit! How could they possibly do
what he did, how could they represent his word with
authority, if they lacked the Spirit with which their
Master was sent out? How could they ever gather
people with Christ if they had not received the Spirit
of his unity with God?

Jesus is gathering! He says clearly: "Whoever does
not gather with me scatters." With motherly protec- Matt. 12:30
tion, he wants to gather the sons of his people in the
arms of his Spirit. His church, like Jesus himself,
resembles the mother hen who unites her children
under her wings. Whoever wants to gather with Jesus
must be of his nature, of his mind, and of his Spirit.
It is both the will and the commission of Jesus Christ
for us to always gather and unite. But this is possible
through the Holy Spirit alone.

Only the Spirit, the Spirit of Christ, can lead disunited people to the united church. No person can do
it – no one is allowed to do it. It must be begun in the

Acts 9:15–17 Spirit and completed in the Spirit. No arm of flesh
and blood receives this authority. Only the Spirit of
the city above can bring the church together. Only
he binds. No human strength is able to do it – no one
may even try to do it. Where the Spirit is building,
no other power is allowed entrance. His building is
erected by his work exclusively. It is completed under
his supervision alone.

> Though men watch, it naught availeth.
> God must watch, his arm prevaileth![10]

He does this through the Spirit. Only under his pro-
Ps. 127:1 tection can his house stand.

The Spirit drives out evil and forgives sins
Every building begins with the work of clearing
up – there must be an empty plot of land for the house
to stand on. When everything is cleared away, the
building begins. No foundation can be laid without
the work of digging trenches and excavating, for every
house must be protected from undermining waters.
Its load has to be tested. Fire precautions are needed.
In times of danger or in a threatening neighborhood,
a watchman is necessary to guard against fire and
housebreaking. The good Spirit keeps evil spirits
away. The house requires protection. The night
watchman patrols it and lets no harm come to it.

The house of the church is protected through
the most watchful spirit of all. The best possible
protection is the elimination of all dangerous powers.
Only the Holy Spirit can clear away everything that
tries to undermine, suppress, or destroy the church.
He drives out all evil spirits. But burdens of the

---

10 Chorus of a traditional German night watchman song, sung every hour
during the night.

past, both old and recent, threaten all believers now.
Powers fought long ago make their old claims again:
they raise their heads in the present, calling to mind
past evils!

How can this destructive power be cut off now if
the point at which it started to develop is not done
away with? The present has its roots in the past.
Only in the light of the past is it possible to cope with
the present. Without the forgiveness of sin, there is
no elimination of evil. The new life cannot begin
if the old is not done away with. The only way the
lame man can be healed is by having the cause of his
illness removed.

Matt. 9:2–7

Christ and his mission destroy the works of the
devil; he takes the ground from under them. With
the power of his liberating Spirit, the church receives
the power and authority to forgive sins. Jesus himself
imparted it to her: "Receive the Holy Spirit. If you
forgive the sins of any, they are forgiven them; if you
retain the sins of any, they are retained." If you take
away a person's sins on earth, they shall stay away
in heaven; but if you leave them unchanged here
on earth, they shall stay a burden in heaven too.
They will keep that person in their clutches with
overmastering power.

1 John 3:8

John 20:21–23

What takes place in the church of the Spirit is
valid in the kingdom of heaven; what is left undone
in her is left undone in God's eyes. No one enters
the kingdom of God without forgiveness of sins, and
without the sacrament of forgiveness there is no
community anywhere. Without constantly renewed
purification, it is not possible to have community
with God or among people. The church must be pure;

otherwise she does not live up to what she should

Eph. 5:27 profess. There is no community other than that of the unblemished Spirit, and this alone is the church. In the authority of forgiveness, the Spirit of Jesus Christ stands by the church as his new creation. He purifies her, as God's monument, from all lack of reverence for what she has to represent.

The church is the Spirit's house

The church is the memorial of the life of Christ, honoring the inmost character of God. The Spirit of consecration acknowledges her as the image of God and with conclusive authority confirms that she is the

Matt. 16:18 rock of truth. Through her foundation in the apostles and prophets, he has entrusted her with everything she needs for her building-up. On the basis of the truth, he commands her to exclude and avoid everything that should be kept out of a consecrated building. This building, this church, is guided with a sure hand. It bears the pure image of God and has a foundation: as the rock building of truth, it is built on

Ps. 118:22 the solid cornerstone, Jesus Christ.

At the end of the early Christian period, the Roman prophet Hermas saw this living monument in a vision and described it in his ninth parable. The Holy Spirit in the form of the church showed him a great white rock big enough to contain the whole world. Its gate shone brighter than the sun, and around it stood virgins clad in white. Stones that had been cleaned and dressed passed through their hands, and with these stones the holiest of buildings was to be built on the white rock. The new gate in the old rock leads into the kingdom of God and to the building that is his church. The master builder

of this rock temple is the Son of God himself. Only
through him is there access to his building. The
pure virgins represent the powers of the Holy Spirit:
through their work, the building becomes one stone
with the firm rock, and through the touch of their
hands, all the stones are filled with the Holy Spirit.[11]
The Spirit is still building his temple. Whoever loves
peace, whoever has a childlike spirit, let them come!
They shall be fitted into the building. Whoever wants
to free every human being from distress, whoever
hastens to do good to all, must be in the temple of the
rock before it is completed.

The Hutterian church has re-established the
prophetic faith of early Christianity. In his first confession, written in an Austrian prison about the year
1530, Peter Riedemann testifies to the same building
of the Holy Spirit, who as power from the Most High
brings about all that is good in his living stones: 1 Pet. 2:4–10
"Through thus revealing and imparting his gift, he
brings together the church and house of God . . .
where [her members] receive forgiveness of sins.
There they are bound together with a band of love as
one body by the one Spirit who brings it all about." In
this Spirit, it becomes clear "how we should build up
the house of God and what the house of God is." Then
"we can begin to build joyfully on the foundation of
all the apostles, whose cornerstone is Christ."[12]

This house is the church of God. Its stability is
in God. The first pillar that supports this house is
reverence for God, which overcomes all fear of men.
The second pillar is the pure wisdom of God, which

---

11 *The Shepherd of Hermas*, 10.4–17.6.

12 Peter Riedemann, *Love Is Like Fire: The Confession of an Anabaptist Prisoner*
(Plough, 2016), 71, 77.

is eternally at war with all human wisdom. The third pillar is divine understanding; on this pillar the folly of human understanding comes to grief. The fourth pillar is the counsel of God, which is bound to contradict all human counsel forever. The fifth is the strength of God in contrast to human force. The sixth is the skill of God as against human skill. The seventh and last pillar is the loving-kindness and friendship of God; against this pillar break the destructive waters that come with love of possessions and a life of pomp and splendor.[13] As in olden times the pillars of the old sanctuary were given symbolic names such as "he lays firm foundations" and "in him is strength," so now the building of the church is in truth founded on the steadfastness and strength of the Spirit of God. Like the pillars of the old temple that stood on silver feet, the pedestals of the seven pillars of the church shine out in the purity of the Holy Spirit.

1 Cor. 1:19

1 Kings 7:21–22

Exod. 36:20–30

God's new temple

All that the dark shadows of the old temple were meant to signify has been fulfilled in the radiant Spirit of Jesus Christ. The house of the old covenant was meant to represent the dwelling of God in the midst of his people. "Have them make me a sanctuary, so that I may dwell among them." To this people, who regarded the old dwelling as the inviolable Holy of Holies, Jesus made a very daring claim: "Something greater than the temple is here." The Holy Spirit dwelt in Jesus as the Godhead embodied in his whole fullness. Jesus placed the true dwelling of God in the midst of men, who despite their old temple were without God in the world.

Exod. 25:8

Matt. 12:6

---

13 Riedemann, *Love Is Like Fire*, 82–89.

Jesus did this in the midst of their hostile unbelief.
When his body was about to be broken, he promised
to restore the demolished temple in three days. And
indeed, he who had risen alive from the dead on
the third day sent his Holy Spirit, who gave the new
temple to the believing church: "The temple of God
is holy; you are that temple." In the quickening Spirit,
Christ and the Father want to come to believing
people and make their dwelling in them, in a new
house of God. The old temple had brought the revelation of God near, yet its nearness was deeply hidden.
In the Son of Man, God's dwelling has come out of its
concealing shadows. In the words and life of Jesus, in
his deeds and in his works, God dwells among men,
visible to all.

John 2:19

1 Cor. 3:17

Col. 1:19

Because of his works, even if nothing else made
them believe, people had to recognize this established
fact: in Jesus Christ the work of God is disclosed by
the Spirit of revelation. His work is his house, the
place where he dwells; he acts from within it. The
Spirit of God wants to enlighten the eyes of all hearts
to see the greatness of his power as it establishes his
work in Jesus Christ. For this reason he sets up a
throne room in the house of the church for the ruler
of the kingdom of God. From here he directs the
embassy sent out by his government. In the church,
the Spirit of God makes Christ, raised to the majesty
of the king of the kingdom, ruler over all things. In
the Spirit, the church can recognize everything given
into her hands from God's kingdom.

John 10:38

Eph. 1:22

The old temple was the tent sanctuary where
people used to gather. Similarly, the church of the
Holy Spirit is the place where everyone gathers

who has a mind to glorify the heart of God and his dwelling among us. Just as God wanted to receive the sincere sacrifices and prayers of his people in the old tabernacle, he accepts the thank-offering of his church in the new temple of the Spirit. Her house is full of jubilation: her Spirit exults to God, and her festivals honor the king. She is filled with such an exuberant joy of the Holy Spirit that out of the fullness of her heart she brings praise and thanks to God, she sings him fervent songs overflowing with the Spirit, and in her whole life and work she honors what his love decrees. The Holy Spirit is the never-failing source of a joy that wells up unceasingly from the innermost depths of the sanctuary and pours out over all lands.

The old temple was divided into the Holy of Holies, the Holy Place, and the forecourts. Its construction showed that most important of all was the center of the innermost place: the further one went from the interior, the more each part of the tabernacle pointed back to the deepest and innermost center and away from itself. God had his dwelling in the innermost place; therefore even this inner covering in the tabernacle was called the dwelling of God. It surrounded the throne that commanded the whole. In the Holy of Holies, the mighty angel-princes testified most powerfully of all to the presence of him who as Lord of the kingdom reigned over them. The princely spiritual beings surrounding the throne of God give it honor and glory.

The throne remains decisive. The death of Jesus Christ has rent the curtain that divided the Holy of Holies from the Holy Place. From now on, God from

Heb. 9:2–3

Exod. 25:17–22

Matt. 27:51

his innermost throne wants to govern, have mastery over, commission, and equip all the forces of the church. The eternal light of the Holy of Holies shines out into the distance. Rulership from God's dwelling flows out far beyond the boundaries of inwardness. It becomes outwardly visible. The place of worship remains in the inner recesses of the house, but the perfect life of the Spirit of Jesus Christ can no longer be limited and hidden. Certainly it will still be true to its starting point in the deepest spirit of the Holy of Holies – that is, faith; certainly it will still keep a certain reserve about its inmost prayers and its dedicated works; yet its aim is to allow the lordship of God's Spirit to grow and expand unhindered. Starting from the Holy of Holies, the Spirit of Jesus strives to gain mastery over all the forecourts.

Thus the whole body becomes the temple of the Holy Spirit. Thus the whole world becomes the parish of his church. Christ dwells in overflowing hearts through faith, and the faith that stems from his love floods over all worlds. As in the Holy of Holies of the old covenant all the vessels, all the walls, and all the coverings were radiant with gold, the color of faith, so the innermost sanctuary of the temple of the Spirit is filled with faith's golden light, radiating far and wide. The faith of Jesus Christ will conquer the whole world. The light of his kingdom will have command over all the ends of the earth. Wherever God takes up his dwelling, the throne from which Christ rules is recognized to be the center of all life.

Rom. 10:17–18

Mark 16:15

1 John 5:4

Eph. 1:15–23

God's Spirit alone shall rule

From the throne of God in the Holy of Holies, all

people were to be ruled. The lost community with
God was meant to be restored from this throne. For
this reason, the forgiveness of sins was proclaimed
from it. For this reason, a sacrifice was needed. But
it is from the throne of the new government that
forgiveness is made a reality. This throne has been
established where a different sacrifice took place,
valid for all time. An ultimate sacrifice was needed;
in no other way could the opposing regime of the
sinister prince of this world be broken. God's new
government succeeds, bringing faith in this sacrifice
of the Lord of Light – a sacrifice unto death that
overturns everything. Then the new certificate of
citizenship is freely given, promising community
between God and his people forever.

The Spirit of the new throne generates a power,
founded on faith in the sacrificed king alone, that
sweeps away everything else. In the all-decisive
battle – his death – he has taken possession of his
throne. His first act as ruler was to declare an
amnesty for all time, which promises his enemies
absolute forgiveness as soon as they are ready to
acknowledge his sovereignty without hesitation. Out
of this faith in the kingly deeds of forgiveness and
the sacrifice unto death, grows perfect love, which is
poured out through the Holy Spirit into the hearts
of the whole people; the Spirit of the king grants to
his people the heart that has his own kingly attitude.
Like their divine king himself, they are able in him to
love – to love God – with all their heart and soul and
mind and with all their thoughts! Like their sacrificed
king, they are able in him to love their neighbors and
all their enemies just as they love themselves! After

Heb. 9:18–22, 26

Heb. 10:10–14

Heb. 11:1

Acts 13:38–39

all, they were only recently enemies themselves! What love they have received! They are filled with its glow:

> The love that points to God in you
> Is God's eternal strength, his fire, his Holy Spirit.[14]

In everything, the new temple proves to be a fulfillment of the old prototype. In the old covenant the congregation used to gather in prayer in the forecourt whenever the high priest bore incense into the Holy of Holies; so now the central fire of the loving church urges the hearts of all believers to gather as one before God. Through enlightenment in Christ, the light with the seven branches is renewed in the seven candlesticks of the church. Christ's fiery love permeates the new life so completely that the bread always offered in ancient Judaism has become, in the new covenant, the surrender of all the means of existence to God's cause. The Spirit of the dwelling penetrates the life of the new house so completely that all it possesses in the way of food or clothing belongs to the one Spirit and his love. The whole house and all that is in it belong to him.

Rev. 1:12–20

Num. 4:7

When the new church is filled with the Holy Spirit it means that, going out from the innermost sanctuary, the whole temple is opened to the Spirit, who rules over everything right down to the utmost use of all the gifts and faculties of every believer in the new covenant. The whole body has become a holy temple. The self-control that makes for the spirit's harmonious mastery of the whole person, right down to all physical urges, is a conclusive fruit of the Spirit. No fruitless branches remain on the tree of

Rom. 8:11

---

14 Angelus Silesius, *Cherubinischer Wandersmann*.

John 15:2–4 the Holy Spirit; he will have nothing to do with them. From all his living branches, love, joy, and peace can be harvested. Unfaithfulness and all impure acts, hostility and murderous hate, discord in the form of bickering and envy, and dissension caused by anger and quarrelsomeness must be kept away from his house just as much as the idolizing of luxury and

Gal. 5:19 possessions. The fruit of the Spirit will not share the same bowl with any dish prepared by the flesh.

It has profound significance that Jesus drove out the bankers with their money tables and middleman's

Matt. 21:12 profits. He did not tolerate them in God's house, not even in the outermost forecourt. Jesus used his sharpest measures against them to win back the outlying forecourt for the house of worship. Like all the outer chambers and rooms in the old forecourt, the whole life of the new church, including the management of all its economic affairs, becomes a holy temple of God through the intervention of the bitter Christ. Once and for all, the power of mammon and all the dealing in money that accompanies private property have been vehemently driven out of the house of God by Jesus.

Our spirit, together with our soul and body, must be kept as a holy temple until the day of Jesus

1 Thess. 5:23 Christ. Starting from the depths of the Holy of Holies – faith – the Spirit of Jesus Christ requisitions all functions and achievements of a life generally stamped as profane. In the forecourt open to the profane, not only the priests and prophets of old but also Jesus and all the apostles of the new covenant represented the truth of the sanctuary. The Holy Spirit wants to spread God's dwelling over all that is earthly and temporal.

The earth is God's. All its gifts and powers are   Ps. 24:1
to be brought under the rule of his Spirit. To do
this, the church of the Holy Spirit was erected in
the midst of this world; her forecourts, dedicated to
God, are to expand over the whole earth. The curtain
is rent. Streams of living water go out from the
innermost sanctuary into all lands. Mighty works of
the Holy Spirit reveal for the whole earth the power
and lordship of the holy throne of God. The Spirit of   John 16:8–11
Jesus Christ has given the new temple of God to the
whole earth.

The church believes in the victory of the Holy
Spirit; she surrenders to his rulership so that God
may be acknowledged throughout the world. She calls
to the Spirit of God to bring the kingdom of Jesus
Christ to all people:

> Far Spirit of the heavens,
> Now lead us in the fight:
> So may we never falter
> But conquer far and wide.
>
> We pray thee, Lord of spirits,
> Lead us forever on;
> We call thee, spirits' Master,
> To consecrate thine own.
>
> Thou art eternal victor,
> Lead thou the feeble band.
> Baptize them for thy service,
> Take thou complete command.[15]

* * *

---

15 From Arnold's poem, "Wir sind so schlecht und niedrig," *Poems and Rhymed Prayers*, 253–255.

The Spirit leads up to the heights.
His name is righteousness.
In him true brotherhood in love
Shall reign throughout all time.

The Holy Spirit, great and strong,
Alone can make us one.
As sword he pierces heart and core –
The Spirit is the truth.[16]

---

16 From Arnold's poem, "Der heil'ge Geist ist gut und zart," *Poems and Rhymed Prayers*, 270–273.